ETERNAL INDIA

CREATED AND PRODUCED BY
EDITA · LAUSANNE

Indira Gandhi

ETERNAL INDIA

Photographs by Jean-Louis Nou

B. I. PUBLICATIONS

Bombay • Calcutta • Delhi • Madras

The captions, written by the photographer, were adapted by the publishers.
English translation by Mavis Guinard

B. I. Publications

Head Office:

54, Janpath, NEW DELHI – 110001

Regional Offices:

18, Lansdowne Road, BOMBAY – 400039
13, Govt. Place East, CALCUTTA – 700069
13, Daryaganj, NEW DELHI – 110002
150, Mount Road, MADRAS – 600002

First Indian edition 1980
First published in English in 1980

CONTENTS

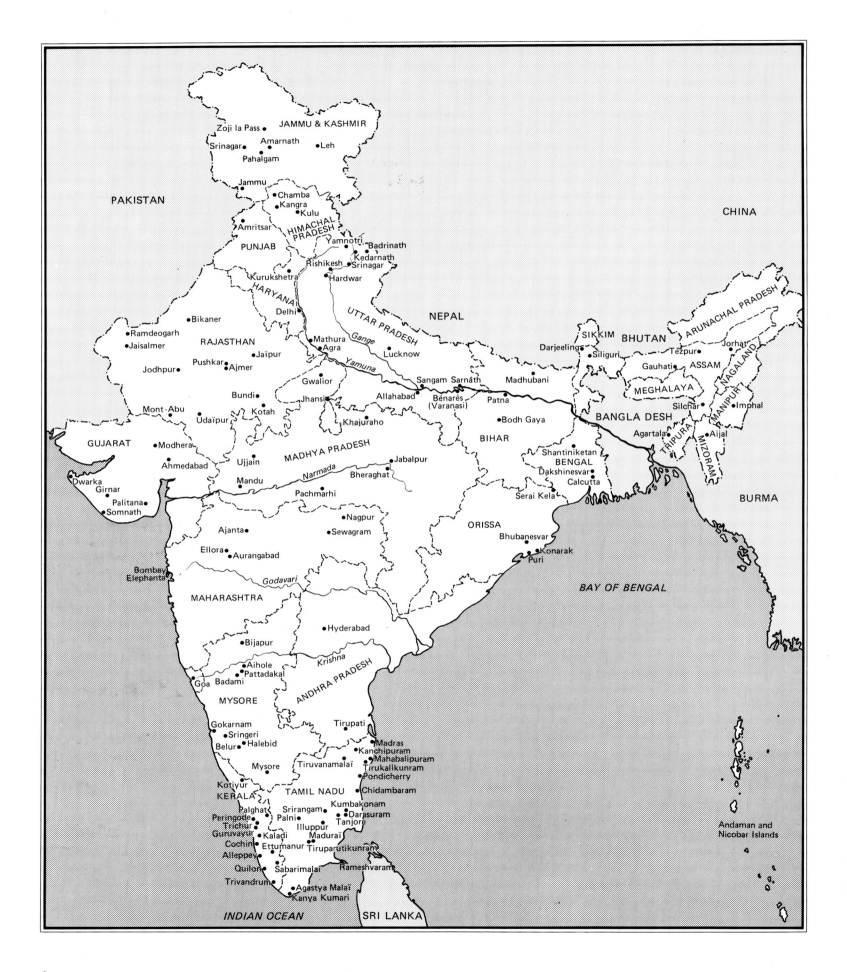

PERENNIAL INDIA

India is a world in itself, it is too vast, too diverse for any complete description. It is in the midst of a great transformation. Indeed, even I who have lived here all my life, travelled many thousands of miles covering known places as well as those difficult of access, I who have met million upon million of our people cannot claim to have seen and understood all, or even most of this extraordinary land. Every journey brings to light some new facet, local legend or contemporary development. No nation has probably accumulated such vast experience or endured so long as a civilization. As with knowledge, the more one delves, the deeper becomes the mystery and one finds that there is much more to know.

What I can do here is merely to point out certain outlines and examples that have helped to mould us as a people.

No country should be judged by the standards of another. Until you discard all labels and preconditioning, India will not reveal herself. India is unlike anywhere else, perhaps not fully within comprehension, yet if you are relaxed and receptive in mind, it is capable of yielding many worthwhile experiences and stimulating ideas. Look beyond the poverty, the heat and the dust to the spirit of the people. What is it that has enabled them to endure when so many other civilizations have crumbled?

The concept of unity is almost as old as India itself. Wise men devised many ways of re-emphasising it, in epics and teachings and by the pilgrimages they enjoined upon us. We have all the religions of the world. But we believe in giving them equal respect. India is a sub-continent with immense variation in geography, climate, manner of life, language and taste.

There is no pure unalloyed Indian. He can be a Dravidian, an Aryan, an Australoid or a Mongoloid. His hair may be fair or dark, straight or curly, the skin very fair or wheat-coloured, beige, brown or ebony. For India has always accepted races, tribes, ways of thoughts and life, without demanding from them conformity which would negate individuality, yet stamping on them the unmistakable mark of Indianness.

Yet the ideals in life, the goal to be reached, the spiritual yearnings and ethical principles bring together these apparently diverse people into one integrated nation that makes up 'Bharat'. The mountains, the plains, the rivers, the forests, the deserts and seas, even these bring together in rare proportion a geographical unit.

Isn't this diversity a marvel and even more so the fact that it has led not to division but to synthesis and unity? Equally wondrous is the vitality that has persisted stubbornly in the face of every kind of hindrance. But our vitality is not the obvious one of muscle-flexing and aggrandisement. It is that more rooted in the profundities of Indian vitality of imperishableness.

The quality of ancient India that is most striking is the breadth of its vision, its capacity to feel at home in vast spaces, to think of great stretches of time and astronomical numbers, a capacity matched only by the mathematicians of our age. The rishis spoke of a day in Brahma's life, a Kalpa, as equalling 4,320 million years. They conceived of a glow that was brighter than a thousand suns. They sang of the circle of birth and death, of creation and destruction, of the many ends which culminated in many beginnings. Obviously they were not men of little minds dwelling in a small land. They reached out to the ever-receding horizons of knowledge. So has Indian imagination questioned easy certainties and finalities.

Through Indian history runs a thread of enquiry by sage, philosopher and king. This fearless search into the inner depths of man's being gave birth to some of the most profound insights of the human race. The extraordinary daring of their speculation is revealed in Vedic literature composed more than 3,500 years ago. One of my favourites is the Rig Veda's Hymn of Creation:

'Then even nothingness was not, nor existence.
There was no air then, nor the heavens beyond it.
What covered it? Where was it? In whose keeping?
Was there then cosmic water, in depths unfathomed?

'Then there were neither death nor immortality
Nor was there then the torch of night and day
The One breathed windlessly and self-sustaining
There was that One then, and there was no other.

'At first there was only darkness wrapped in darkness
All this was only unillumined water.
That One which came to be, enclosed in nothing.
Arose at last, born of the power of heat.

'In the beginning desire descended on it—
That was the primal seed, born of the mind.
The sages who have searched their hearts with wisdom
Know that which is kin to that which is not.

'But after all, who knows, and who can say
Whence it all came, and how creation happened?
The gods themselves are later than creation;
So who knows truly whence it has arisen?

'Whence all creation had its origin,
He, whether he fashioned it or whether he did not,
He, who surveys it all from highest heaven.
He knows—or may be even he does not know.'*   * Translated by A. L. Basham.

The tribals, the ancient inhabitants of the land, had their own myths of creation. It is interesting to compare the two.

'In the beginning there was nothing but water, water, water. There was neither voice of God, nor of ghosts, no wind, no rocks, no paths, no jungle. As the sky is now, so was water then. On a great lotus-leaf that drifted here and there on the water, sat Bhagwân. There was no fruit or flower to his life: he was alone. One day he rubbed his arm, and with the dirt that came off he made a crow, his daughter, Karicag. When she could fly, Bhagwân said to her, "Go and find some earth for me, I am lonely here; I want to make a world."'

Scholars acknowledge the ancient Indian's capacity for clear abstract thinking which was responsible for numeral notation and the decimal system of numerals. In the sixth century, Âryabhata in his Âryabhatîya, one of the earliest surviving mathematical treatises, presupposes an earlier knowledge of this system of notation, which was to become the basis for all mathematical discovery. Who the discoverer was is not known. But there is no doubt that from an early date such profound mathematical concepts as the zero and infinity were understood and used in the material sciences as well as metaphysics. Professor Halstead writes:

'This giving to airy nothing, not merely a local habitation and a name, a picture, a symbol, but helpful power, is the characteristic of the Hindu race from whence it sprang. It is like coining the Nirvana into dynamos. No single mathematical creation has been more potent for the general on-go of intelligence and power.'

Dharma or the ethical mode of life has dominated Indian thought. Philosophy has deepened and widened the people's outlook and helped an affectionate approach towards not only fellow beings but towards all nature, especially animals, birds, trees and plants.

Like India herself, Hinduism is incapable of confinement or description in words. It is a philosophy, all-embracing, all-accepting, tolerant of other thoughts, giving vast freedom of choice in worship. The manner of it and even whether there need be any at all—is God a being or the divinity in man or the force or quintessence of all that is? In the Gîtâ, Krishna in the form of God describes himself, 'I am the sceptre of rulers, the strategy of the conquerors, the silence of mystery, the wisdom of the wise.' 'I am the seed of all being. No creature can live without Me.'

Hinduism is not an 'ism'. There is no prophet, no book, no dogma. The much discussed myriads of gods and goddesses are but different images of the formless, all-pervasive 'energy' of this universe and many others beyond it. Through the ages, within the Hindu fold sages have broken away from any kind of crystallisation. Some founded sects and even new religions, offering greater liberty to those who felt, or were made to feel, fettered and suffocated.

Does our religion stand in the way of progress or modernisation? I would say no, contrary to some beliefs, for the great majority of Indians are by and large down to earth and not opposed to change, which they realise is beneficial to them. In all of us there is something of both strands. Thus even in the mind and habit of the scientist, science and some kind of superstitions co-exist. But can we not say the same of the Western or industrialised world? Have not the most violent iconoclasts set up new gods?

One must admit that large numbers think of religion in terms of idols, and Indian practice has not always lived up to the precepts laid down. At different stages, large segments of our society have surrendered to intolerance and insolence. Customs or rites still persist which may have had some significance in an earlier age but are now anachronistic or even actually obstruct progress. A case in point is the caste system.

Yet in its philosophical groundwork, Hindu society does not aim at exclusiveness. From this has risen India's unrivalled capacity to accept and assimilate. It is also true that religious people respect and accept the saints and great souls of their religions. Hindus, Moslems, Christians, Sikhs will go with equal fervour to obtain the blessings of a Shankaracharya or a famous Moslem divine. When His Holiness the Pope came to Bombay in 1965, millions of people of all religious beliefs flocked to the airport for his blessings. You will often see a church, a mosque, a temple, a gurdwara all on the same road or in the same vicinity.

India is a land of contradictions but basically isn't every developed human being so? Can one even know another human being fully? How so a country? India's seeming lack of sophistication is the result of centuries of spiritual evolution: the wisdom of countless saints mingled with experience of vast political upheavals.

Our myths and legends are not stories of the past but experiences that are lived and relived by each successive generation, very much part of our daily lives. Everyone quotes examples from them and the epics to illustrate a point or draw a moral. It is not uncommon for our unlettered peasants and others who have never heard the names of the poets to quote couplets of Kabir or ask a riddle of Khusrau's. In Srînagar, I have heard a boatman singing a song of Queen Habba Khatoon (sixteenth century) as he paddled along. That is why I once said that our people have a cultural literacy.

Poverty has not soured the Indian. It has chastened him with a spirit of acceptance which is very different from resignation. There is no despair. On the contrary, he has learnt to feel and create beauty in the most adverse conditions, to make his own entertainment and music, to join in dance. Even the poorest are hospitable, going out of their way to welcome the unexpected or unknown guest.

Cultural enjoyment has been a great factor in Indian life. But the roots of all great arts, having their source in the village temple as an offering to the Almighty, were understood and appreciated in the farthest nooks and corners before they reached the centres of sophisticated excellence in aesthetic intake. Music, dance and drama, painting, sculpture and architecture, crafts and every other branch of aesthetic expression had a wide appreciative audience, whether in the village or in the town. The folk idiom was as much in vogue as the classical.

India remains deeply rooted in her past that she loves so well, but is equally receptive to the most modern discoveries that have revolutionised life, without losing her balance in taking in both: India has always been an enigma.

One of our best known prayers is:

'From the unreal lead me to the real
From darkness lead me to light
From death lead me to Eternal Life.' *

* From Brihadâranyaka Upanishad.

10

THE
PURIFYING
ABLUTIONS
THAT BEGIN
EACH DAY

'The daughter of Heaven has appeared with the light:
Young woman in flaming garb,
Who reigns on all the earth
Blessed dawn, shine on us today.' Rig Veda. I. 113.

At dawn and at dusk, the faithful bring to the river offerings of flowers, fruit and tiny oil lamps to float down the current.

'Here comes the light of day, the most precious light of all: the radiant messenger is born in all his might.' Rig Veda. I. 113.

Dawn, the daughter of Sky and Sun, announces to the faithful it is time to salute the appearance of the celestial body by lighting the oil lamp at the river's edge and greet the Sun God *(Surya Namaskara)*.

'O Divine Gangâ,
who has come to this
earth, hear my praise,
O Mother of Waters.'

Standing on the ghat (steps), the believer contemplates the river Gangâ (our mother the Ganges) then,
holding out his hands over the waters, he pronounces the 'Gangâ mantra' (symbol of the divinity).
Then he takes water in the palm of his right hand to drink; bows to the four points of the compass, the
guardians of space, and concentrates on pranayama (fixing his thoughts by controlling his breath).
Finally, he immerses himself in the waters that Hindus believe the primordial element.

Following double page:

'Just as the waters of the Ganges and Jamuna are mingled, so are mingled in the heart of the seeker after truth, the twin currents of love and sacrifice.

'Through his heart, flow the sacred waters night and day and so ends the cycle of deaths and rebirths...'

A father plunges his young son in the water, three times in succession. It is here in Kashi, city of light, that the linga of water is worshipped and that this sannyasin (renouncer) of the Siva sect has come to worship the statue of Siva Nataraja. Mythology tells us that Gangâ, the celestial river, descended to earth to bring life and calmed its impetuous current in the matted locks of Siva.

After immersion, palms joined towards the east, the Brahman lets water drip between his fingers as a sun offering while reciting the mental formula of the triple-chant (gayatri), guardian of all primordial energies. Water is used in all the rituals, in various degrees, as an element of purification: the faithful offer libations to the gods, to the wise ones and to the souls of the departed, or offer milk to the waters as a symbol of fertility and plenty.

DAILY LIFE
IN HARMONY
OF DHARMA

If the wind that has caressed the waters of the Ganges touches a man's skin, it takes away any evil he might have committed: such is the virtue of the sacred river as it is sung in the epic chant of Mahâbhârata. The ascetic, seated in a lotus position facing the Ganges, paints on his forehead three horizontal lines of sacred ash (Bhasma).

Roughly speaking, India is heart-shaped. The magnificent Himalayan range rests like a coronet on its north and the waters of two mighty oceans caress its long shoreline on the two sides. Kâlidas writes in his 'Kumârasambhava', 'In the north lie the abodes of Gods, the kings of mountains—the soaring Himalayas. The waters of the oceans embrace it on its eastern and western shores. It stands as a measuring rod of the earth.' From their eternal snows down to the southernmost tip, from the west to the east and within the long coastline, the area is 3,280,543 kms. There is every type of climate, flora and fauna of the temperate zone as well as the tropics.

For an agricultural community, water is life. That is probably what gave rivers their sanctity. Bathing is a ritual and also a purifying experience. Jawaharlal Nehru paid homage in the following words: 'The Gangâ specially, is the river of India, beloved of her people, round which are intertwined her racial memories and her hopes and fears, her sense of triumph and her victory and defeat. She has been a symbol of India's age-long culture and philosophy, everchanging, ever-flowing and yet ever the same Gangâ.'

The myth of its emergence at Gangotri describes the earth's desperate need for fresh water, accompanied by an apprehension that the force of the river's descent might annihilate the land and the people. To break the fall, Siva as a symbol of the Himalayas, holds the water in his matted locks.

The Gangâ with its clear water and her sister river Jamuna of the dark water have been flowing for millennia on millennia through our northern plains. They have moulded the lives, habits, arts and cultural norms of the people who live within the fertile Ganges plain. At Prayâg—modern Allâhâbâd—the rivers mingle and become one. Millions converge to bathe at the confluence during the 'Kumbh Melâ', a religious gathering of great importance. Thus united the Gangâ flows onwards, past ancient Kâshi, the Vârânasi of the Buddha's days and our own, until it reaches the rich plains of Bengal. Just at the mouth it is joined with the vast Brahmaputrâ that has travelled the north-eastern route from Tibet. And now the journey over, this great stream becomes one with the sea. To many in India, these rivers symbolise the life of man, the birth, the maturing, the storms, the vast risings and ebbings and finally the merging into infinity.

Between these majestic heights and the plains are other ranges on which there is habitation, although living conditions in the higher region are terribly hard. This region gives us our pine nuts. A little lower come the orchards of pears, apples, peaches, almonds and walnuts, and many other fruits.

Across the heart-lands of India lie the heavily forested Vindhya highlands. The uneven walls of caves became the picture gallery for primitive man. In recent years, a large number of rock paintings and drawings have been discovered depicting man as the hunter, the shaman, man dancing, and also animals, bull, elephant, deer and horses are etched, apparently so alive, so abounding with energy.

From the highland of the Vindhyas and the Sahyâdri ranges arise the Narmadâ, Mahânadi, Godâvari and the Krishnâ rivers. The Kâveri is amongst the holiest rivers of the south. In the west are the deserts of Rajasthan and Kutch. Their starkness and the everchanging patterns of the sands have their own eloquence. Perhaps as a compensation, the dress of the people and the cloths used to cover animals are vibrant with colour. The women wear wide-swinging skirts, bangles which cover the lower and upper arms and much else besides. The men's turbans are yards and yards long. There is richness in the embroidery, in the indigo and alazarine dyed cloths, and in the intricate wood-carvings and other creations of the artisan. In sharp contrast to the dryness of most of North India, is the eastern area whose landscape is verdant in every tone of green. Here is located the wettest spot on earth. Most Assam houses have their mulberry trees and the women folk weave all the cloth the family needs. To protect themselves from the strong sun and the no less strong rain, the peasants wear huge (they can be as large as umbrellas) hats made of bamboo.

Very different again is the gentle beauty of the tropical south. Flowers are brighter, trees are much larger or else elegant like the pencil-slim areca palm. This is the area of spices. Here we have our plantations of tea and coffee, cocoa and rubber, pepper and cardamom. Adjacent to the sea are the fresh backwaters shaded by coconut groves. Along the sea-shore, stretch some of the world's finest beaches with many-hued sands. Perhaps because of the lushness of the landscape, traditionally the men and women wear mostly white. Only in the dance costumes of the south does one see vivid colour.

Goa on the western shore was under the occupation of the Portuguese. It is full of beautiful old churches, one of which boasts the body of St Xavier. Pondicherry on the east coast resembles a typical old-fashioned small French provincial town. French is still spoken, especially in the Sri Aurobindo Ashram which has encouraged people from all our States and many countries to come and settle in a new city— Auroville—to which they have brought handfuls of soil from their own areas.

Taking the old sea route to the Indies discovered by Vasco da Gama at the end of the fifteenth century, heavy boats loaded with precious spices, salt and coconuts slide through the waters of Lake Vembanad in Kerala.

India is as large as Western Europe. There is a theory that if India had not come under colonial rule it might have been a cluster of many independent nations like Europe. But I doubt this. At various stages of history, India has been a single political unit—during the reign of the Mauryas, the Guptas and the Moghuls. And even when a score or a hundred rival kingdoms battled with one other, the people thought of themselves as belonging to one country and one civilisation. The people of the far south have always regarded Benâres on the Gangâ and Badrinâth in the foothills of Himalaya nearly 2,000 miles north, as their own cities. The people of the north have the same feelings for Râmeshwaram and Kanyâ Kumârî, the southern-most point.

Virile nomadic people migrated over the length and breadth of India, intermingling with the original inhabitants. Vast civilisations met and were absorbed into one another. Alien myths and Gods met and interbred with archaic gods, ancient nature divinities and cults connected with fertility, the earth and harvesting. Cosmic perceptions and the earth-bound nature-rituals created common myth and Godhead. No religious impulses were rejected. And out of this integrating urge and intention arose a way of looking at life that had a niche for all living things.

This unitary vision did not arise through conquest, but with a merging of races and cultures, the acceptance into the Brâhmanic ethos of large numbers of indigenous people through the 'Vratya Stoma' ceremony. For in the early beginnings, caste and class were flexible.

A special characteristic of Indian life is its rhythm, and a subtle law that determines this rhythm. Rhythm governed by law produces harmony. This is the harmony which one discovers in India. Indeed, this is the harmony of Dharma, to use the Indian subtle concept of the law which is not a result of legislation but has emerged from the profound truths of the growth of men and creatures and their interaction with the total reality of the universe, vibrating with the élan of evolution.

At the root of the social structure, in art, in craft, in daily acts of life and in attitudes towards nature and life, one finds Dharma, even though the deeper sense of Dharma is often distorted or obscured in outer forms and expressions.

Early societies all had their hierarchies. Caste of one kind or another has been known in all old lands. In India caste became a set feature of life. People were divided into four groups: priests and scholars, kings and warriors, traders and landowners, and workers. In the early beginnings there was caste flexibility. Inter-marriage between the Aryans and the indigenous people appears to have been common. The children of these marriages gave rise to mixed castes.

Another factor responsible for the proliferation and crystallisation of the caste structure was the establishment of craft guilds. Initially there was fluidity which made possible the absorption of people within their structure.

This was common as late as the sixth and seventh centuries. An inscription of this period at Mandasaur in Rajasthan records silk-weavers who had migrated from Gujarat, taking up professions ranging from soldiering to astrology. In early Tamil literature there is no evidence of caste.

By the late medieval period the caste structure had hardened, the lowness or highness being determined by the functions in which the group was engaged. What is worse, a large segment of the population was placed beyond the pale of these varnas (as castes were called) and sentenced to untouchability. The Hindu mind, which discovered the zero, also invented a system by which the human being was reduced to a zero. Indescribable injustice has been visited upon the so-called untouchables through the centuries. The only extenuating plea that can be made for India is that in other lands such groups would have been killed off but here they were not extirpated.

ARTS AND CRAFTS

One cannot imagine India without her art and her handicrafts. Both are closely linked and continue to be an integral part of rural life and still most of India lives in its villages.

Rural art expresses itself through functional objects, in the print or weave of cloths, in pots and other utensils, in the many kinds of baskets and other articles of daily use, and in the architecture of huts. Another element is the purely ornamental, the gestures of joy and love to bring pleasure to God and man. In almost all parts of the country during marriages and births and other auspicious occasions, designs or geometric patterns are made, for example the Warli in Mahârâshtra or the delightful Madhubani paintings of the women of Mithilâ which depict episodes from the epics and old legends. What flights of imagination, checked tigers, fantastic abstract shapes! Sometimes a touch of sophistication creeps in the midst of utter simplicity. Women smear cowdung on the floors of their huts and with finger tips and the palms of their hands make designs of great precision, vitality and beauty, or draw patterns with lime-mixture, with grains or flowers. They weave garlands of mango leaves and marigold and other flowers to hang at the entrance to their huts or on the dewlap of bulls at cattle fairs—bulls with horns painted with indigo or turmeric or madder red. The most versatile items of decoration, also used for various ceremonies, are the coconut and banana plants. Henna is said to be cooling and women apply it to their palms and soles. It is a fine art and experts can trace very delicate designs in a few moments. It is a must for weddings and other auspicious events.

The art and artifacts of our tribal people are directly linked to tribal cults and the worship of archaic gods and primeval nature deities. All tribals delight in ornaments for their body, carved hairpins and combs, bright coloured beads and cowries for necklaces and for pouches and boxes to hold tobacco and other items. The design framework is geometric, angles and triangles emerge sharply.

Classical art grew in our sacred centres and around the court and temples of the early kings. The guilds of artisans were responsible for the creation of division between fine arts and handicrafts. Every facet of life and creative expression was integrated and rooted in function. Objects were made for religious worship, for patrons, for trade and also for daily use. Designs were rich in symbol and myth. The artisan's anonymity did not lessen his concern for beauty of form which was perfected not as a conscious effort, but out of an innate feeling for line and colour and an unequalled understanding of functional needs and the problems of materials and technology. The child of the craftman grew up in his workshop, exposed to the work of masters of material, technology and form, so his education was part of a living process.

Each region has conserved its own craft form. The artisan was not an imitator, this is shown in the artisan's capacity to absorb new forms and ideas into the idiom of his technique. Indian craftsmen travelled to South-East Asia. The innumerable invasions that entered northern India brought in their wake a stream of master craftsmen. With the establishment of Moghul rule, new elements, new approaches and new dimensions were introduced into the design consciousness of the craftsman and his relationships with his source of vision, his materials and his tools.

While India produced many goods, it was for her textiles that she was most famous and continues to be known. Some 5,000 years ago a cotton cloth called Sindu was being exported to Babylon and Baluchistan.

There are superb specimens of wood-carving in temples and houses in Gujarat, Rajasthan and Malabar. All forms of metal work in bronze, copper, brass, bell-metal and silver are also ancient crafts which continue to supply the domestic market. The unglazed earthenware tradition of pottery moulded on the wheel by the village potter is of very ancient origin. The shapes, techniques and decorative motifs are lovely and simple and have remained unchanged from the time of the Indus Valley civilization. Terracotta images of animals and gods are moulded for ritual purposes and displayed at village shrines. Clay toys are popular at village fairs.

The last twenty-five years have witnessed the emergence of new trends in crafts and art, music, dance, theatre and films. On the one hand, there is search for roots and the discovery of symbols that give tone and sustenance to our cultural identity and, on the other, a revolt against all static solutions and a groping for new media through which to express the anguish and the alienation as well as the laughter and joy of our people. The creative spirit is alive. It delves deeply, breaking through and extending the horizons of perception and meaning. Traditional art forms and the modern artists challenge each other, but a dialogue has begun in which the folk and the contemporary are seen as two sides of a coin, both fully relevant, both interpreting through living eyes and hands, the India of today.

DAILY LIFE

The average person's daily routine naturally depends upon the part of the country in which he lives. But wherever he may be, earning a living and looking after the household, it is closely linked with religion and festivals. The day begins with a bath and, no matter how busy or how early, with prayer which may vary from region to region and even from home to home, since traditions peculiar to the family are built up over the generations. Moslems offer prayer (Nimâz) five times a day. Most Hindu houses, however humble, have a Tulsi plant which is offered flowers etc. The days of the week belong not only to the planets, but to specific gods. Women are of course in charge of the kitchen and food plays an important part for guests and in worship, for offering to the gods. Festivals call for special menus and so do fast days. Fasting does not necessarily mean not eating, merely avoiding items such as cereal or salt or sour things. The variety of the cuisine matches the size of our country. On the whole, Indians like spices and sweets. People who live in the mountainous regions as well as on several coasts eat meat. In the coastal areas fish is a basic item. Even carnivorous Hindus do not eat beef and Moslems do not taste pork. Vaishnavism, the worship of Vishnu, brought in vegetarianism widely. But the strictest are the Jains who will not touch root vegetables or anything that is red or remotely resembles meat. Hands must always be washed before prayer and before eating. This is natural since we eat with the right hand. A Persian emperor is said to have explained to Queen Victoria that eating with a knife and fork was like making love through an interpreter.

INDIAN WOMEN

Our mythology has a rather beautiful concept of the 'ardhanarîshwara', a half female, half male combination to make the perfect whole: Siva and Shakti. In referring to a divine couple, the name of the female is always taken first: Sîtârâm, Râdhâkrishna, Gaurîshankar, showing the high position reserved for the female.

The Vedas asserted: 'The wife is the home.' In spite of other handicaps, the mother usually does rule over her domain. In the West, the mother-in-law who is the butt of jokes is the wife's mother nagging her son-in-law. But in India the traditional picture of the mother-in-law is far from funny. Alas, she soon forgets her own tribulations as a young bride and often bullies her daughter-in-law, who has to do much of the work. Women in the south have a higher status and are more independent because of the matrilinear system. In the north, women are more backward in the erstwhile Indian States. Polygamy used to be practised before Independence. In some hill regions there is polyandry. In the Mahâbhârata, the five Pandava brothers share a common wife Draupadi who, unlike the gentle Sita, more than held her own with all of them.

The first woman of India, or probably of anywhere in the world, to think of women's liberation and equality as we do today was Chitrâ of the Mahâbhârata era. She was a princess, the only child of the king of Manipur. As she undertook all the arduous tasks of an heir, she became rather rough and unfeminine. But one day she espied Arjuna the Pândava prince, one of the heroes of the Mahâbhârata, hunting in the forest. Chitrâ fell desperately in love with the handsome prince, but despaired of catching his eye because of her own plainness and lack of appeal. She beseeched the goddess to grant her beauty for just one year and indeed she was transformed and Arjuna was bewitched. No one recognised Chitrâ in her new guise. She was ecstatic, but the administration suffered, the people of the State felt unprotected and missed her and wondered where and how she had disappeared. Arjuna's interest was held by the many tales he heard of the princess's valour and ability. He yearned to meet the famous princess. Chitrâ decided to reveal her identity and her original form. Then it is that she says to Arjuna: 'I am Chitrâ. No goddess to be worshipped nor yet the object of common pity to be brushed aside like a moth with indifference. If you deign to keep me by your side in the path of danger and daring, if you allow me to share the great duties of your life, then you will know my true self.'*

Laws and customs in India, as indeed in other countries, are made by men. In ancient times women enjoyed full freedom and equality. They were philosophers, such as Gârgî of the Upanishadic period whose questions touched the very frontiers of knowledge. Sanghamitra, daughter of Emperor Ashoka (second century B.C.), was the first missionary, undertaking the long and perilous journey by road to a port on the east coast and thence by sea, in order to carry the message of the Buddha's teaching to Ceylon. One of the great twenty-four Thirthankars, the great teachers of the Jains, was Malli, a princess of Videha, later known as Mallinath. Leelavathi assisted her father Bhâskarâchârya, who was an eminent mathematician.

Unfortunately, as the structure of society crystallised, this status changed. Manu (seventh century), lawmaker of the Hindus, had some kind words to say about women but these seem to be by way of a sop to compensate for firmly relegating them to a secondary position in society, completely subservient to their menfolk. Inevitably, some women did break these bonds. Razia Sultana reigned as queen of Delhi in the thirteenth century. And we have Mirâbâî, the rebel saint princess of Chittor, who left home to lead the life of a mendicant, wandering about expressing her love for

* From Tagore's 'Chitrângadâ'.

Krishna in songs of her own tender composition. Lakshmî Devî wrote a great commentary on the Mitâkshara.

Where outside India could one find a woman such as Ahilyâbâî. Deeply religious and renowned as a saint, when she assumed the regency of her State (Indore, Central India), she proved to be an able administrator and a courageous general in battle. Two other women who have captured the imagination: Rânî Lakshmîbâî of Jhânsi in the north and Rânî Chennammâ of Kittur in the south. They both died while fighting the British. The English general who opposed Lakshmîbâî called her the 'best and bravest of the rebel leaders.' She was just a young woman of twenty then.

In our own times, it was Mahatma Gandhi who visualised woman power and its use in his non-cooperation movement. It was a giant step in women's emancipation. There was a tremendous upsurge and arousing of social consciousness. Women of all classes and castes, from town and village, sophisticated as well as illiterate, came alongside their menfolk to take equal part in the political and constructive programmes of the Congress Party in our struggle for independence. They did not expect to be nor were they spared any hardship. The Indian National Congress had three women Presidents even before Independence: Annie Besant, Nellie Sen Gupta and Sarojini Naidu. In 1959, I was the fourth.

India is indebted to many foreigners. Some gave us a deeper understanding of our own ancient philosophy at a time when our colonial rulers seemed to have convinced us to deny its worth, thus rekindling the embers of a dominant national pride. Others loved India as their own and identified themselves with our problems and served our people with rare devotion. Most notable amongst the women was Annie Besant, a woman of great character, the first woman President of the Indian National Congress. She was a suffragette and took a very prominent part in the Home Rule Movement and was put under house arrest. She did a great deal for education, especially women's, establishing schools and colleges. An ardent theosophist, she became President of the Society and was responsible for the movement's gaining momentum in India.

Nellie Sen Gupta, another Britisher who made her home in India and became immediately involved in the freedom struggle, was made Congress President when her husband, the then President, was arrested. A brave woman, after Independence she chose to stay on in East Pakistan in spite of personal difficulties and separation from her family, in order to sustain the morale of the minority communities, the Hindus and tribals. Until she died, she remained deeply concerned with the people and their problems.

Margaret Noble, who took the name of Sister Nivedîtâ, was the first western woman to be received into any monastic order in India. She was initiated by Swâmî Vivekânanda.

Sarojini Naidu, the fiery Bengali poet, whose large-heartedness, eloquence, charm and wit captivated all who met her, was intensely feminine. She had an avid interest in people and their lives. She lapped up gossip, had a passion for beautiful saris, enjoyed good food and was brimming over with fun and liveliness. After Independence, Mrs Sarojini Naidu became Governor of U.P. She was ideal for the job and it was largely due to her benevolent and reassuring presence that U.P. was free from communal trouble in the grim days following the partition of the country.

There are thousands of examples of typical Indian women who emerged from the shelter of closely guarded family lives, straight into confrontation, not only with political oppression but face to face with the crudest elements of society. For Gandhi allotted to them the task of picketing liquor shops and those selling foreign cloth. They showed enormous and unexpected courage and ability in holding various Party posts when more and more were arrested. How then could they be kept back from later endeavours? There was no need for a special movement for women's liberation. There was no conflict between men and women since both were engaged in a common struggle. Jawaharlal Nehru was an ardent supporter of women's rights and was mainly responsible for opening up greater opportunities for their increasing involvement in national affairs. At Independence, women got the vote and soon afterwards the right to inheritance and divorce. Now they are also entitled to equal pay. No vocation except the defence forces is barred to them. Women of character have made their presence felt on the domestic scene and whenever afforded the opportunity have proved their capacity in whatever position they have occupied.

Partition brought much misery and devastation in its train, but it created conditions in which hundreds of thousands of women who had lost their husbands or fathers had perforce to stand on their own feet and earn their living. Almost overnight the social taboo against women of good families working for money was swept aside.

Women have always been involved in social welfare work. Now new opportunities opened out for them and dealing with these problems, starting new schemes and programmes gave them poise and self-confidence.

Many women have come to the fore. Some have been women governors, judges, ambassadors, besides the large and increasing number of those who are working at all levels of politics, the administration, in business and the professions. In the rural areas, women are elected to village councils as chairmen or members.

In legal reform, as in other spheres, several centuries of evolution have been compressed into a couple of generations, with the result that social laws are ahead of actual practice. Thus there is a lacuna between the legislation for women's rights and the social sanctions required to make the legislation a reality.

Woman is the conserver of tradition, but she is also the absorber of the shocks of the future. Therefore, she must be a bridge and a synthesiser. She should not allow herself to be swept off her feet by superficial trends nor yet be chained to the familiar. She must ensure the continuity which strengthens roots and simultaneously engineer change and growth to keep society dynamic, abreast of increasing knowledge and sensitive to fast moving events. The solution lies neither in fighting for equal position nor in denying it, neither in retreat into the home nor escape from it. The approach must be positive. The development of a 'total' personality, which is constantly enlarging its area of awareness, a personality which because of its contact with reality and its courage to tread new paths and through sheer force of character, compels attention.

On the coast of Coromandel, fishermen's wives collect the shells that they will thread into delightful, bright necklaces. On the coast of Malabar, at Kerala, sailors dry their morning's catch in the village street. Young girls play on the beach and skip over the waves.

◁The first monsoon clouds snag on the peaked summits that frame the Zoji la pass, leading to Ladakh. Ahead of the snow that will block the high Himalaya valleys for eight long months, a shepherd leads his flock into the valley of Srînagar.

Rama told the wise men: 'When, in another age, I will be reincarnated in Krishna, you will be reborn as the daughters of shepherds and will know of love with me.' *(Krishna Upanishad.)* At Mandu, the ancient capital of Malwa (now Madhya Pradesh), a young girl takes the buffalo to pasture. Behind the field are the ruins of the fortified castle of Baz Bahadur. Not far from Dwarka, in the Gujarat, a shepherdess of the Bhill tribe squats in the midst of her dogs, guardians of her flock.

◁As the fires are lit for the morning meal, a peasant in the region of Madhubani (Bihar) leaves for the fields.

Vegetarianism spread under the Buddhist influence: just before the monsoon, the young rice shoots are planted in the irrigated fields of Tamil Nadu. Two hundred years before Christ, the Greeks were astounded by the fertile Indian soil and praised the skill of the farmers: all the village women have gathered to pound the rice in rhythm to their chants. In the eighteenth century, English settlers developed tea-growing. Here a young woman picks off the two tender leaves at the tip of the plant.

A peasant plucks the flowers of a kadamba. One day, Krishna mischievously stole the saris of his milkmaid companions as they bathed and hung them from branches of a kadamba.

At the beginning of the Keralite year (in April-May) a farmer ploughs his first furrow in the direction of the East, towards the rising sun. (Peringotukurussi, Kerala).

In order to celebrate the return of spring, each village woman of the Madhubani region, Bihar, decorates the walls of her dwelling with naive designs.

In the Tamil Nadu, Kanchipuram is the city of temples and silks: women spin on the doorstep. Still dripping from the copper dyeing vats, the skeins are hung up to dry by the dyers. Lengths of woven turbans dry in front of a painted house at Jaisalmer.

An Indian woman lives each day to the rhythm of water: in every town, they are ready to tip the copper pitcher to give water to the passerby. The women of Somnath (Gujarat) gossip as they gather at the village well. In the desert of Thar, at Mohangarh, a Rajput village woman goes to the well. In the inner courtyard of the Darasuram temple (Tamil Nadu), two young women fill up the heavy bronze jars.

Small craftsmen sell their wares from their doorsteps. Vermilion powders for makeup and offering, glass bracelets of many colours are spread out in the streets of Benares for passersby. At the entrance of the temple, village women prepare flower garlands for offerings (Pushkar, Rajasthan). Visitors flow continuously by the Eastern gate into the long corridors of the temple of Minakshi. Families stop to buy souvenirs or fruit for offerings.

A religious objects salesman in a sidestreet leading to the temple of Pashu Pati (Siva, as lord of the animal kingdom) offers the pilgrim a choice of white marble linga (Siva's symbol).

The wheel that symbolizes the ever-recurrent cycle of existence, is found in daily life in the potter's wheel of Shantiniketan (Bengal) or in the smithy of Jaipur.

The song-guide recently adopted by singers has become a popular instrument. At Sanganer, a village close to Jaipur in Rajasthan, traditional methods are still used to manufacture paper.

'O Ram, I will perform all trades.
Deep in the absolute, I will no longer fear death,
I will become a potter and make clay pots.'

Poem by Kabir.

The tailor prepares a carpet with colourful hand-blocked designs.
A sculptor carves the statuette of a god.

Indian craftsmen are gathered into corporations. The associations stimulate in the best workers and merchants group spirit and professional pride. With few tools, the Indians reach a high technical level. A stonecarver chips out of a block of marble a likeness of Mahavira, founder of the Jain religion. The puppet makers show the popularity of this typical Rajasthan art that tells the tales of chivalry. This goldsmith, who has been given the title of craft emperor, engraves a gold-and-enamelled elephant and in Rameshvaram, workers restore the temple paintings in the halls leading to the sanctuary of Siva.

A young woman goes out to wash her laundry from the doorstep of her home protected by a likeness of *Ganesha*, the elephant god.

Under a *pipal* tree, particularly revered in India where it is thought to be the tree of life, villagers gather for the morning bath. (Pushkar, Rajasthan).

Sheltered under their palm-leaf parasols (gosa), Nambudiri Brahmins leave for the bath, long before day break, at Poomulli, Kerala.

'Friend, tell me who is that unknown with the golden skin?
I saw her bathing at the ghat.
On the banks of the Jamuna, she was seated, legs crossed in the water, on the sari she had just taken off.
A golden necklace hung on her naked breasts, like the tips of hills of Sumeru.
On the banks of the Jamuna, she wrung my heart just as she wrung out her red sari and ever since, peace has abandoned my fevered heart...' (Chandidas).

Morning ablutions in Palghat (Kerala): each morning the Malayali women bathe in the river. Traditionally, the women's ghat is separate from the men's, as here in Arattapula.

After the morning bath, a young Brahmin woman of Nambudiri, dressed in a white sari, puts on her marriage necklace (Desamangalam, Kerala). The wooden architectural details are typical.

The Ratirahasya of Kokkoka, written in the thirteenth century, says of woman: 'Until the age of sixteen, a woman is called a bala (child); until thirty, she is taruni (young); from then until the years that are counted by the five arrows and the five stings of love, she is pradha (mature). From then on the woman is aged (vrddha).'

In her kitchen, a Nambudiri Brahmin woman churns butter in Desamangalam (Kerala).

A Rajput woman spins thread with a decorated distaff.

In the Malabar, September is likened to a woman bearing a jug of water on her head. The rains of the monsoon are over, the new harvest is in, the sky is bright with the light of the month of Chingom. Everyone celebrates the monsoon festival: young girls wear hibiscus flowers and dance the kaikotikali in Desamangalam.

Each year, in Kerala, everyone waits impatiently for the return of Emperor Mahabali, a legendary king who was defeated, a long time ago, by Vishnu and allowed to visit his lost kingdom once a year. He is welcomed by intricate arrangements of flowers, oil lamps, designs drawn on the ground and small clay pyramids.

On the threshold of the house, young girls of Nayar choose the freshest flowers to decorate the manda-la in honor of the feast of *Onam*: scarlet java, yellow champa, gandha in shades of white, yellow and red, as well as the blue aparajita; nor do they overlook delicate mallika and the fragrant malati. During the Diwali festival recalling the crowning of Rama (October-November), the mistress of the house offers rice balls to the domestic cow. Every spring in Mithila, the women repaint the floral designs around the doors of the houses. In Kanchipuram (Tamil Nadu) women trace over the votive drawings with rice paste (rangoli). At Madhubani, in the Mithila district (Bihar), village women paint scenes from the story of Krishna, the blue-god revered here in North-East India.

The Ganguar feast is celebrated in March in Rajasthan in honour of the Goddess Gauri (one of the names given to the wife of Siva). The young girls who want to marry ask the goddess to fulfill their wishes. They offer her water in which they have steeped kusha grass, an aromatic plant called 'flower of immortality'.

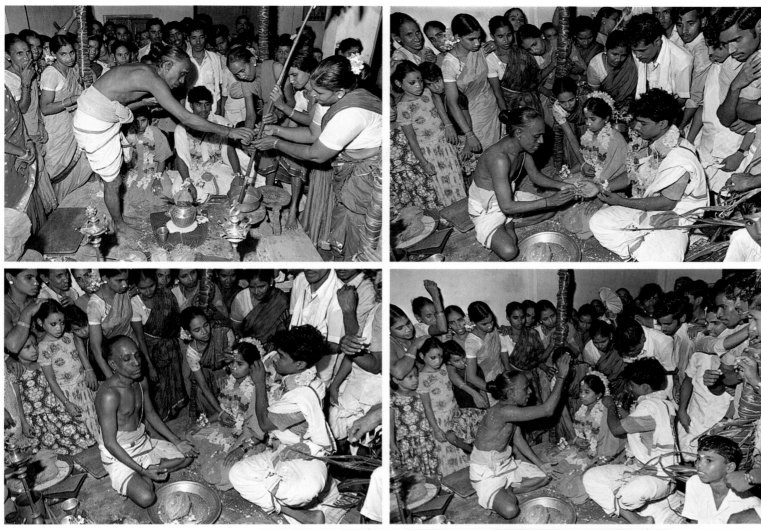

The religious marriage ceremony is usually arranged by the families after consulting with the astrologers and studying the auspices. For the most part, people marry within the same caste or the same class. The ceremony that is conducted by the village priest lasts for several days and follows precise rites. One of the most important celebrates the union of the partners at a hour set by the stars. On a raised platform, the priest lays out all the objects belonging to the cult, clay jars filled with sacred water and the beneficial elements. The groom pays homage to the earth's blessing by presenting a lighted oil lamp before a copper pot containing mango leaves, rice, coconut, a symbol of regeneration and cosmic fertility. Each act of this ceremony is intended to link the young couple: the young man applies to the forehead of his bride the vermilion paint that proclaims her newly wedded state, passes around her neck the marriage necklace (mangal sutra): onlookers throw rice, and the couple joins hands over a plate of coconut, symbol of fertility.

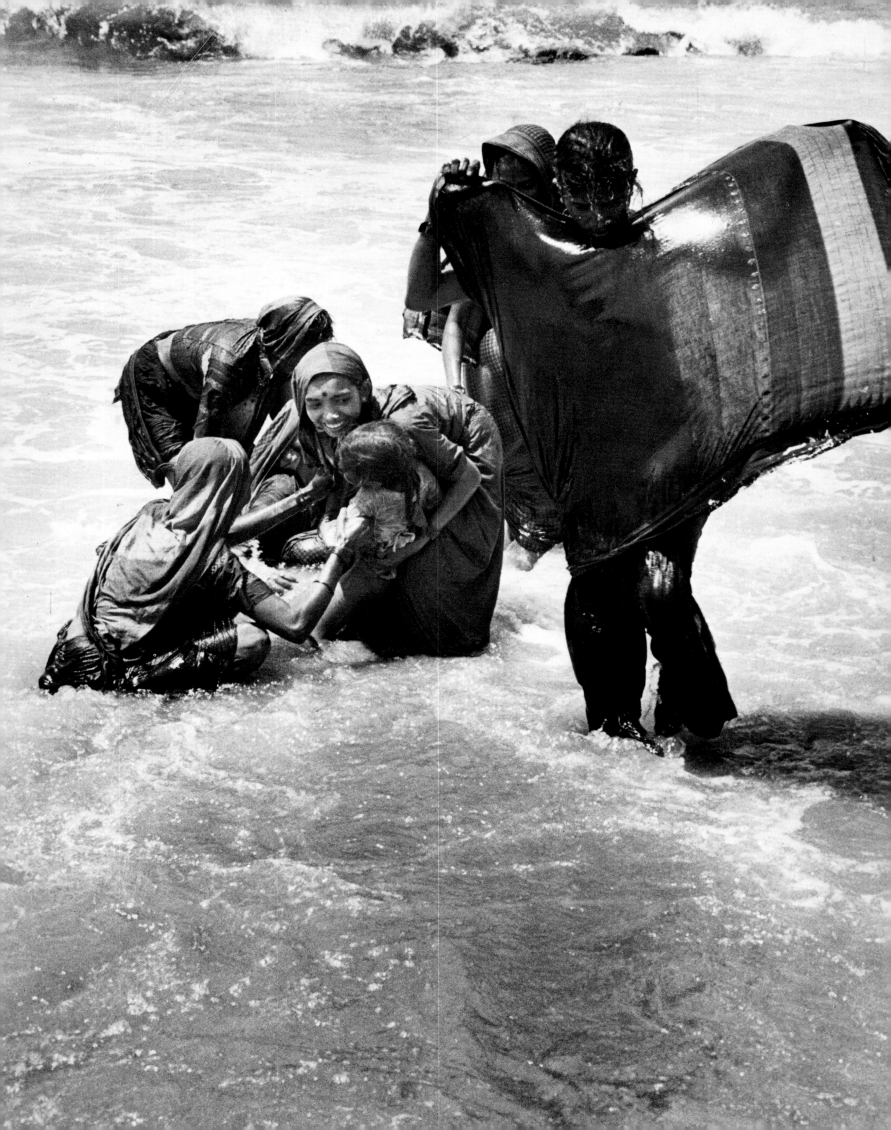

FOUR STAGES
OF LIFE

Indian ethics laid down four main ends to man's life—Dharma, Artha, Kâma and Moksha. Dharma is a difficult word to translate. It means that which sustains or upholds, a way of life resting on right action, respect for others and being true to one's self-nature. Artha was the earning of wealth by a right and honest vocation. Kâma was the fulfilment of lawful desire or pleasure, and Moksha was liberation from rebirth by the perception of the ultimate reality.

With these were also linked the four stages or âshramas of man, essential for a full and meaningful life. Brahmacharya covers the beginning of adolescence and includes the practice of celibacy, the study and the knowledge of the sacred teachings transmitted by a Guru. Grihastha, when man married, had children and undertook the responsibilities inherent in the life of a householder. Vânasprastha, the first step towards moving away from the life of the householder and preparing the mind and body for the withdrawal from all wordly pursuits and for the involvement in social and religious action. Sanyâsa, the final stage, when man put on the saffron robe, abandoning home, family, wealth and society, and entered the forest to meditate and seek liberation, before his ultimate departure from the earth.

Most Hindus believe in reincarnation. All human beings and other living creatures are reborn as a result of their past actions in other lives. Higher beings come on the earth by a voluntary action in order to face a special situation. In the Gîtâ, Krishna says, 'To protect the righteous, to destroy the wicked and to establish the kingdom of God, I am born from age to age.'

Young women bathe a little girl in the sea.

65

No finite experience can fulfill a human being's aspiration for the infinite. In answer to man's need to learn, to enjoy, to understand and finally to become detached, Hinduism offers four stages in man's existence that allow him to accomplish his life in harmony with Dharma (the law of universal harmony) at all levels.

During the first stage, the child will discover, at the time of the feast of Vishnu (the Keralite New Year), all the earth's blessings gathered together in a bronze bowl; an older woman of the family will be his teacher, as here at Jodhpur (Rajasthan).

Before presenting him with the sacred cord (upanayana) that is the outward sign of his belonging to the first caste, a Sivite teacher shows a young Brahmin how the libations to the gods are made: the statue represents Vishnu. In all the regions, Vedic schools teach the young Brahmins to recite the Veda by heart.

In the gardens of Poomulli, ▷ Kerala, a Nambudiri Brahmin reads a sacred text.

As a religious student (brahmachari) the young disciple (shishya) will receive his religious instruction from a Brahmin chosen to be his teacher (guru). In the courtyard of the temple of Varadaraja Swami (Vishnu, as giver of blessings), in Kanchipuram, master and pupil both bear on their foreheads the distinctive sign of their sect.

A brahmachari (student) sits in contemplation in the dancing hall of the temple of Varadaraja Swami in Kanchipuram. Morning, noon, and night, each day he repeats (japa) the Gayatrimantra.

'...We meditate about the blessed light of the sun
that illuminates our minds...'

The head of the house offers gifts to the divine Mother (Bhagavati Puja) represented on the floor by designs made of coloured powders and rice paste in Guruvayur (Kerala).

The name garhasthya, the second stage of life, is given to family life with all its duties and responsibilities. In India, religion is practiced mostly within the home; the family, in the evening, as here in Desamangalam (Kerala), makes the offering of fire to Krishna-Niranjana.

The married man tastes life and founds a family: the Brahmin eats his meal served on a banana leaf (Kerala).

At Kaladi (Kerala), where the great theologian Shankaracharya was born, Brahmins celebrate a couple's sixtieth marriage anniversary.

When he is older, man enters ▷ into the fourth stage of life: he may retire from the world, meditate, study or live as a recluse or a hermit in the time allotted to him before he dies. The head of the house waters a *tulsi* (basil) plant consecrated to Krishna, at Kendubilva, birthplace of the Bengali poet Jayadeva who sang of the infinite grace of Krishna-the-blue-complexioned god.

'...When a man dies, his heart glows and his soul goes forth through the eye, the skull or some other part of the body...'

'...Just as a caterpillar, when it reaches the edges of a leaf, moves on to another, so the soul as it leaves the worn-out body moves on to another...'

A cremation ceremony is held in the presence of the men of the family at Poomulli, Kerala.

CULTURAL LIFE

India has a great heritage of classical dance and music. The classical traditions of all regions derive their basic inspiration from the sage Bharat's analysis and his treatise on the aesthetics of dance and dramaturgy. The main classical forms are: Bhârat Nâtyam, a stylised dance originating in the temples of South India, its poses immortalised in the sculpture of many temples. It has regional variations, such as Kuchipudi of Andhra and Odissi of Orissa. The Kathak dance from the north was also originally inspired by religious themes, but this changed during the Islamic period and it became a popular court dance with a more exuberant style, emphasising footwork and pirouettes. The tiny State of Manipur in the north-east is distinctive in many ways. Its classical dance is very gentle, ritualistic and restrained and there is evidence of affinity with the dance of South-East Asia. By contrast, the men's dances are most energetic.

The Kathakali of Kerala is dramatic and intense. In elaborate costume and make-up, the characters act themes of valour and heroism from the epics to spellbound audiences.

Indian classical music claims the Vedic chants as its source. Indian music is not written and cannot be learnt from books. Traditions of music have been handed down by teachers in a special master-disciple relationship. The Islamic influence introduced flexibility and a certain lightness to our classical music. The two broad categories of classical music are the Hindustani music of North India and the Carnatic music of the south. Amongst well-known instruments are the veenâ, sitâr, sarod, sârangî, shehnâî, flute and different kinds of drums and percussion instruments.

We have a wealth of folk dances and songs, closely interwoven with the lives of the people. Almost all age groups participate. The tempo varies from the slow and languorous movements of the tribal and hill regions to the staccato movements of the Mizo bamboo dance, to the boisterous leaps of the robust peasants of Punjab, the splendour of the colourful whirling skirts of Rajasthan, to the disciplined and virile movements of the Nagas. Folk songs are sung on almost all occasions but, broadly speaking, the themes are occupational or connected with ceremonies, festivals, and the changes of seasons. Ballads are more often about tales of heroism and romance.

The classical traditions of our theatre have been lost. However, forms of folk theatre continue to thrive in different regions. It is fascinating to watch the spontaneous rapport with the audience. Folk traditions have been the main vehicles for transmitting our traditional values through the acting of tales and legends from our epics as well as any contemporary theme which may have aroused the interest of the local people.

PLASTIC ARTS

From the terracottas of the Indus Valley civilization to the expressionist work of today, India's sculpture has had an interesting evolution. In each century and in each region are revealed new stylistic developments and subtleties in expressing the basic idiom of the period. Besides famous temples such as that of Konarak to the Sun God, some of our best sculpture is in the caves of Elephanta, Ellora and Mahabalipuram in Tamil Nadu.

Mural painting reached new heights in Ajanta and the tradition continued for many centuries with changes of style in other regions. Parallel with this emerged a tradition of manuscript illumination. The Persian school of miniature painting introduced by the Afghans and the Moghuls enriched this art and various schools flowered in the north and the Deccan.

The modern phase of Indian painting is much more contemporary than our other art forms. It is experimenting with the universality of meaning through abstraction as well as the primitive and spiritual symbolism of our own milieu and traditions.

Architecture can be said to have followed an almost similar pattern, starting from the splendid temples, viharas and town complexes to the influences of the Islamic architecture which reached its zenith at the time of the Moghuls, and finally to the contemporary architecture of the technological age. Traditional designs of village huts made of bamboo or palm, cane or sun-dried clay or conifer have proved to be the most practical and inexpensive, besides using locally available material and being in harmony with the landscape.

E.B. Havell has written, 'That Hindu art was successful in its educational purpose may be inferred from the fact, known to all who have intimate acquaintance with Indian life, that the Indian peasantry, though illiterate in the western sense, are among the most cultured of their class anywhere in the world.'

Centuries have given to the Indian a way of feeling space, a way of creating form—an integrated approach to art. But there must be constant awareness, a renewal in terms of contemporary challenges. Only in this renewal can a tradition remain rich and alive. With its open-heartedness in absorbing new ideas, India was bound to become a synthesis of many cultures.

LITERATURE

The Vedas and the Upanishads set the tone for our later literature. Vedic hymns movingly expressed awe of and sensitivity to the beauty of nature. This appreciation runs like a thread throughout Indian literature, from the early epics and plays of Kâlidâs down to the modern works of Rabindranath Tagore.

The earliest literature is mainly in Sanskrit (meaning civilized) which was the language of the elite. Buddhist and Jain literature was in Pali. Classical Sanskrit literature reached its high point in the earlier centuries up to 900 A.D., when great writers like Kâlidâs, Bâna, Bhavabhûti and others perfected the language, chiselling it into a fit vehicle of superb drama and sonorous poetry.

In order to reach a wider audience, saint-poets in different parts of India sang in the spoken languages, often in a homely style, laced with humour and satire. Their compositions transcended caste and other barriers. This gave an impetus to regional literature. In the south, the ancient language of Tamil and other languages continued their rich traditions.

In the latter half of the medieval period, northern India was influenced by the advent of Islam, when Persian with a strong admixture of Arabic and Turkish words became the State language. Out of this was born the Urdu language whose power and grace added another dimension to our literature.

The modern age of Indian literature begins from the nineteenth century and was influenced by European thought. This impact also created conflict by awakening political consciousness. Bengali writing was the first to be deeply imbued with fierce patriotism and social awareness.

Our freedom struggle inspired our writers and they in turn sustained our faith in our movement and our goal. Gandhi and other leaders laid special emphasis on regional languages. Tagore brought new life to Bengali and inculcated a sense of pride in his mother tongue. Other languages also continue to gain in richness and strength and are producing much fine writing. Good work has also been done in the English language.

The contemporary epoch witnesses a renewal of interest in the tradition and research in its profound origins. But, at the same time, one notes the influence of modern literature. India has always considered that violence and sex are a part of life, but society defined certain taboos. The modern writer is more liberal as far as his subject and style are concerned. He seems to have overcome his inhibitions; the reference to sex is more conscious, one could almost say that he has a desire to be shocking.

Mahadevi Varma, born in 1907, a mystic poet of Allâhâbâd, represents the modern period of contemporary literature of the Hindi tongue.

In Southern India, the ▷ Malayali painter K.C.S. Panikker was the leader of the impressionist movement, then of painting of tantric inspiration. Not far from Madras, he founded an artist community—Chola Mandal—where new artistic tendencies find their expression.

Firaq Gorakhpuri, a poet of the Urdu tongue. Allâhâbâd.

Jamini Roy (1887-1972) has ▷
been one of the masters of
modern Bengali painting.
Most of his inspiration comes
from ancient or folk art, like
the paintings of the Kalighat.

At the beginning of the century, Rabindranath Tagore and Nanda Lal Bose created a new style of
painting: using water colours, they focused on Indian themes and experimented with techniques
inspired by the Moghul and Rajput miniatures or the Ajanta frescoes. From their findings developed
the Bengal school. In Shantiniketan where Tagore used to live, the cultural tradition is kept up by
numerous artists, like the sculptor Ramkinker and the blind painter Beenod Behari Mukerjee.

Following double page: According to ancient legends, the gods revealed music to the sages who then passed it on to man. In Benares, the city of music of Northern India, Pandit Kishan Maharaj plays the *tabla* and Gopal Misra, the *sarangi*.

The Sanskrit word, sangita, means music: it includes song—gîtâ—instrumental music—vadya—and dance—nritya.

The music of India is most varied and expressive. Its rules are based on ethical and metaphysical principles that must be observed to obtain good music and that are, for the musician, the sign of his human quality. The instruments are highly sophisticated: top, left, Narayana Swami, playing the vina, lute of the South (Trivandrum, Kerala).

Song plays a fundamental role in music; lower left: two of the masters of Karnatic music: Semmangudi, Srinivas Iyer and Chembai Vaidyanatha Bhagavathar, taken during a recital in Madras. The violin, though recently brought into India, has been adopted by artists of the South, such as V.V. Subramanya.

A member of the oboe family, the *shahnai* is an instrument of marvelous quality of sound, very difficult to play. Bismilla Khan, from Benares, is the most famous shahnai virtuoso.

Shrimati Kishan Maharaj tunes the *sitar*, an instrument whose origins lie in the fourteenth century. Sharan Rani plays the *sarod*.

The Karnatic singer of Madras, M.S. Subulakshmi accompanies her song on the *tampura*, a four-stringed lute.

Siva taught men to dance and play instruments. Indian dance has not changed throughout the centuries. The great masters still observe the rules of the Natya Shastra. Bala Sarasvati, a dancer of Bharata Natyam—the classic dance of Southern India, formerly danced in the temples in honour of the gods. Rukmini Devi, dancing mistress, with her pupils in Madras.

Certainly one of the most common forms of theatre in India, the Cakyar kottu still represents today the Sanskrit drama in its purest version. For over fifteen centuries, a few Cakyar families of Kerala have passed on the tradition of this pantomime. During the yearly village festival in front of the temple, before a gathering of brahmins, under the wooden frame (kuttampalam) an actor plays, in Sanskrit, the part of the king's buffoon (vidushaka).

◁ Chatur Lal, tabla player in Northern India.

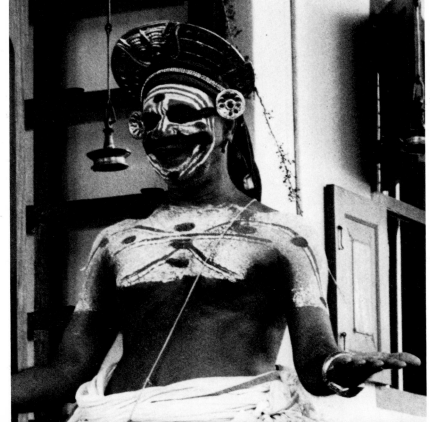

Dance (nritya) is closely linked to the theatre (natya). The dancer must express himself with his entire body: every movement is practised for hours on end and must be under perfect control—whether it is the lifting of an eyebrow or a finger. The pantomime expressed by the hands (mudra) together with the expression of the face (abhinaya), allow the full development of the nine emotions (navarasa).

Up early, young dancers practice in the enclosure of the temple of Guruvayur (Kerala). On the walls are frescoes of the Goddess Durga, mounted on a lion, fighting the demon buffalo, Mahishasura; on the right is the popular monkey-god, Hanumân.

One scene shows the demon Putana trying to poison Krishna as a baby by feeding him at her breast.

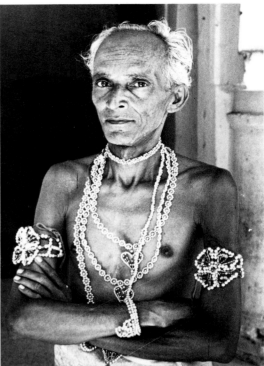

The Chhau dance was quite recently created by the Maharajah of Seraikala, near the Orissa and Bengal borders. Dancers wear masks made by the village artist under the instructions of the ballet master (above right). The characters are taken from traditional Indian legends (lower right). Right page: a dancer as Chandra, the moon.

RELIGIOUS LIFE

A tragedy to be danced by a single actor, the ottan tullal was written by Kunsan Nambyar (1704-1781) in its present version. The danced and recited stories derive from the epic poems and the *Purana* or from certain Kerala legends.

Millions of Hindus begin the day with a prayer to the Sun contained in this Gâyatrî Mantra:

'Om, let us meditate on
The radiance of the Divine.
May it inspire and illumine our intellects. Om.'

The religious ethos of India was given flexibility, tolerance and strength by the absence of a single religious doctrine, based on a 'bible' or sacred dogma; by the multiplicity of forms and faiths that collectively formed India's religious beliefs and the Vedic and break-away traditions of our sages and seers. It was an inclusive attitude, drawing the alien heretical belief within a total ambience, extending and absorbing while respecting the beliefs of other religions. Heresy was unknown and religious persecution was minimal.

From the earliest times the Indian has envisaged a continuum between God and Nature and Man. The gods were human, but godhood was inherent not only in man but in all animals and in all creation animate and inanimate. In the words of the Bhagwad Gîtâ, 'All gods lead to God as all rivers lead to the Sea'. And again it was said 'Truth is one, the wise perceive it in many ways'. This recognition of the possible limitation of one's own viewpoint, this hospitality to the opinion of others, this refusal to condemn mankind to a single interpretation of Reality, this high reverence for the quintessence of Truth as distinct from phenomenal forms demonstrates a marvellous maturity of thought. This is the source of much that is most distinctive in our civilization and also, I think, the secret of our endurance.

The first millennium B.C. was a period of abounding creative activity. The sacred worship of the Upanishads, where the sublime thinking of centuries coalesced and found expression, treads beyond priestly dogma and belief. Anti-theology and anti-ritual, the Upanishads established a new relationship between man and the Brahman, the all-transcending principle. 'As flowing rivers go and rest in the ocean and there leave behind their name and form so likewise the knower released from name and form goes to the divine man, who is beyond the beyond'. The Svetâsvatara Upanishad says, 'Man may try (through his technical advances) to roll up the sky itself as if it were a piece of leather; but with all that, he will never succeed in achieving peace and the end of his sorrows without realising the luminous Divine within Him.'

After the Upanishads came our great epics, the Râmâyana and Mahâbhârata. **EPICS** Their influence on the masses has not diminished over the centuries. They continue to enthrall grown up and child alike. In fact, we can say that the heroes of these classics have blended with the lives of our people. Typical of India is their method of reaching out simultaneously to different levels of mental development, from the intellectual to the illiterate. Their stories have been a kind of open university, quickening our people's sense of right and wrong, and endowing them with examples with whom they can identify themselves and exalt their moral sense. Through a backdrop of heroic tradition and ethical living, these classics give harmony to a society which was graded in castes and had many divisions and discords.

Of the two Epics, the Râmâyana is the much more popular, presumably because it is easier to understand. Tulsidâs has translated it into Hindi and there are old versions and adaptations in other regional languages.

Writing in 1864, Michelet, the French historian says of the Râmâyana:

'... Everything is narrow in the West. Greece is small and I stifle; Judea is dry and I pant. Let me look towards lofty Asia and the profound East for a little while. There lies my great poem, as vast as the Indian ocean, blessed, gilded with the sun, the book of divine harmony wherein is no dissonance. A serene peace reigns there, and in the midst of conflict an infinite sweetness, a boundless fraternity, which spreads over all living things, an ocean (without bottom or bound) of love, of pity, of clemency. I have found that for which I searched: the Bible of kindness.'

The Râmâyana centres around the hero Rama but there are many subsidiary stories, each with its own moral and significance.

The Mahâbhârata is a treatise on the science of society. It is a monumental work, a compilation not only of tradition and legend but also of the political and social institutions of that time.

Sister Nivedîtâ (Margaret Noble) writes about the Mahâbhârata,

'The reader ... is at once struck by two features: in the first place its unity in complexity; and, in the second, its constant efforts to impress on its hearers the idea of a single centralized India, with a heroic tradition of her own as formative and uniting impulse.'

It has been pointed out that the Mahâbhârata makes a very definite attempt to stress the fundamental unity of India. India was called Bhâratvarsha after Bharat the legendary founder of the race.

What is important about the Mahâbhârata is not the story which concerns a feud between the Kaurava and Pândava princes for the sovereignty of the country but the sheer abounding wealth of knowledge and the fullness of life, no less than the moral and ethical precepts. The lesson of the Mahâbhârata is a timeless one.

In the Mahâbhârata is a gem of a poem, the 'Bhagwad Gîtâ' or the Song of God. It is an epic poem. William V. Humboldt describes it as 'the most beautiful, perhaps the only true philosophic song.' The wisdom of the doctrine of the Vedas, the Brahmanas and the Upanishads come together in this teaching. It is the most important and the best known of all Hindu scriptures. The Gîtâ comprises a dialogue between Krishna 'the Lord who abides within the heart of creatures' and Arjuna, one of the five Pândava brothers, of whom he is the friend and charioteer. The Gîtâ expounds the nature and attributes of God. Its teaching is universal and deep. It is a general spiritual philosophy as applied to a specific crisis and relating to the application of ethics and spirituality to the problems of man. In simple language, Krishna explains the imponderable truths that are the basis of Indian religious thought.

The Gîtâ teaches three ways to realisation and union with the absolute: Karma Yoga is the way of action, Bhakti Yoga of devotion and Gnana Yoga of intuitive insight. The way of the Karma Yogi is to act rightly and fully within the world, without caring for the fruits of action, equable in victory or defeat, pleasure or pain. Action that is not rooted in motive, frees man from the effects of actions: 'Action rightly renounced brings freedom. Action rightly performed brings freedom. Both are better than shunning of action.'

The way of devotion is the way of love, when man putting aside all duties, all relationships, all desires surrenders and takes refuge in the Lord. The true devotee is beloved of the Lord:

'Whatever man gives me in
True devotion,
Fruit or water,
I will accept it.
That gift is love
His heart's dedication.'

The path of insight is when self-knowledge and Yoga frees the mind of all impediments, such as desire, thought and the fire of becoming, and rests illumined in self-knowing.

Although the paths propounded are three, essentially they are one, the freeing of man who is in bondage and who lives in illusion. Krishna says, 'He is illumined who is free from craving, neither shaken by adversity, nor striving after pleasure, free from lust, free from fear and anger. He is the seer and the illumined.'

Through the centuries Indian religion has grown richly and deeply psychological, and has attempted to provide different forms and methods appropriate to different categories of people. There is the spiritual man, for whom Indian religion provides an utter freedom from all dogma, ceremony and creed. It offers him numerous paths of direct experience of the spiritual verities. There is the intellectual man, to whom are offered different systems of knowledge, countless philosophies and unending literature of commentaries and of commentaries on commentaries. There is the vital man, the man of emotion, passion and action, for whom there is a vast literature of stories, *Kathâs*, a plethora of accounts and practices, as in *Purânas* and *Tantras*, which will stimulate his imagination and experience and connect them to the deeper truths of the spirit. And finally, there is the physical man for whom Indian religion is a system of outer symbols and rituals, of festivals and other such occasions which, even in his daily routine, bring him into contact with the deeper truths that govern the cosmos. It is in this light that the complexity of Indian religious life can rightly be understood. The cults of Nature and ceremonies of Temples have their own superficial and profound significance, although many of them are discouraged by those who feel able to pursue the deeper and higher disciplines of emotion, action and knowledge.

THE WORSHIP OF NATURE

The worshipper who contemplates Siva, here in the form of Linga, may only reach the Master who is the very 'nature of the sky' by removing from his body any trace of desire or earthly attachments.

Pouring the lustration on the Siva linga at Seraikela, Orissa.

Krishna and *Kaliya*, king of serpents are represented on this propitiatory stele. Such steles are venerated in all the villages of Southern India, specially by women who want a child.

The love of trees is so strong, specially among Indian women, that they are regarded as companions. The 'kalpavriksha' or tree of blessings is deeply rooted in Indian belief. Offerings of fruits, flowers and sweets for his proverbial sweet tooth are brought to elephant-headed Ganesh or Ganapati—the son of Siva, god of prosperity—in his shelter under a *pipal* tree.

Under a *pipal*, a priest from the temple of Chamba (Himachal Pradesh) first offers Hanumân, friend and servant of Rama, the symbol of faithfulness, jasmine flowers, then pours lustral waters on a votive stone. In its most elementary stage, any sacred spot in India consists of a tree (the symbol of life), a stone (representing the sacred mountain, centre of the Universe), and water (primordial element).

At Prabhaspatta, in the Gujarrat, the place where Krishna is believed to have abandoned his body to rise to heaven, the *pipal*, surrounded by a low wall of white marble fretwork, is adored as a divinity.

'In the heart of the waters, O king Varuna,
Your golden home is built.'

(*Atharva Veda.*)

In India, the river is considered as a loving mother dispensing bounty, fertility and prosperity. The cult of rivers is specially important: at Dwarka, a family performs the preliminaries of an offering (sankalpa) under the guidance of a priest. In the sacred pool of the temple of Venkateshvara (one of the thousand names of Vishnu), a couple purify each other, because water is the very essence of life, the first element created in all the universe.

In the poem of Raghuvamsa (13,9), poet Kâlidas describes the ocean '...as a painter caressing his wives the rivers, drinking from their lips and giving them in exchange draughts of his water...' In Dwarka, a holy city where Krishna is said to have reigned, a group of pilgrims pay homage to Samudra, the sea.

The sea, in the Indian cosmogony, is the reservoir of all.

In Somnath, fishermen's wives honour the departed.

Bathing in the sea is considered the most purifying since all the sacred rivers run to the sea.

In Rameshvaram, Tamil Nadu, a priest pours sea water from a coconut shell over the hands of the faithful. A couple, with knotted clothing, emerges from a purifying bathe to go to the temple.

110

'Fine, fine cloth, delicately woven.
Of what is made the warp, of what the weave?
What threads went into its weaving?...'

Poem of Kabir.

Women dry their saris in the wind, following a ritual bath, on the terrace of 'Shore Temple' of Mahabalipuram (Tamil Nadu).

THE LIFE OF THE TEMPLE

In India, there are as many temples as gods who conceived the world. But for the Indian, the temple is not the only place of worship of the divinity. Even if the sanctuaries disappeared, the religious life would not change an iota: the temple of the Hindus is at the same time the entire universe and their own bodies.

In the Hindu concept of existence (Sanathana Dharma) there is no separation between sacred and profane activity.

Young women entering the temple of Chidambaram dedicated to Siva Nataraja (Lord of Dance). On the walls of the great portal are sculpted the various positions of the Bharata Natyam, Southern India's traditional dance.

A testimony of faith and fervour of devotees, the entrance towers (gopura) of the impressive temple of Madurai, dedicated to *Minakshi*, rise against the sky. The temple is the centre of the cosmos as well as of man. Believers come to render homage to one of the major figures of the Indian pantheon or to seek the protection of the god of their choice.

'When he has by all his acts worshipped the gods, man acceeds to deliverance.' *(Bhagwad Gîtâ)*

The two main rites are individual worship (puja) and ritual sacrifices (yajna). The rites are a most complex and painstaking art. First of all, by repeating the sacred words, the worshipper, like this widow with her head shaven in sign of loss and penance, must become one with the god.

The first part of the rite is to purify the worshipper, under the guidance of a priest who supervises the ceremony (temple of Lakshman, near Rameshvaram, Tamil Nadu). A family undergoes the rites of purification. After three immersions, they will return to the priest under the colonnades (temple of Chidambaram, Tamil Nadu).

Pages 118 and 119: Each adores his particular god: 'When one of my faithful wishes with true fervor to adore me under a particular form, I immediately assume that form.' *Bhagwad Gîtâ* (7,11). To attract the blessings of the god, worshippers in the temple of Tiruparuttikunram (Tamil Nadu) throw little balls of butter, a prosperity and fertility symbol, at the feet of a statue of Durga. Before entering the Holy of Holies, the worshipper prostrates herself before Vishnu veiled by the yellow pitambara. 'The dark body glistens through this golden veil, just as the divine reality shines through the sacred verb of the *Veda*'. Temple of *Brihadisvara* in Tanjore.

There are a number of symbolic gestures in all the rites. 'The idea of worshipping images is to venerate the invisible through what is visible...' The rite of purification performed, the young woman pays respect to the older woman by wiping the dust off her feet and carrying it to her forehead (Temple of Tirupati, Andhra Pradesh).

At Rishikesh, the faithful cluster at the door of the temple. A temple is usually entered by the East gate after paying respect to the guardian gods of the sanctuary. 'One must enter a place of worship with the right foot.' But here in the temple of Kali at Dakshineshvara, one enters with the left foot for all the rites are performed with the left hand (Bengal).

Siva's mount is the bull (vrisha), often called Nandi or Nandikeshvara (Lord of happiness). In any Siva sanctuary, near the figure of the god is represented his mount. Before entering the heart of the sanctuary, the worshipper pauses to touch the hoofs of Nandi, that signify justice, righteousness, virtues of the strong. As they come closer to the sanctuary, the faithful ring a bell to attract the attention of the gods and bring them down to earth. Before the sacred precinct of Bajri Shri (an epithet for Indra, king of gods) the faithful worship the divinity at Kangra (Himachal Pradesh).

'By listening and repeating the sacred hymns that sing of my glory, the spirit is purified.' *(Bhagavata Purana)*

Other worshippers are seated in meditation. As they forget the outside world, the god will fully appear to them.

120

'There are images of eight kinds, of wood, of stone, of metal, of pottery, and of precious stones. They may be painted, or exist simply in the mind.' *(Bhagavata Purana)*

Offerings of flowers and coins to a representation of young Siva dancing with joy (Padmanabha).

Siva, the god who moves the world, is worshipped and covered with fragrant garlands at the temple of Ujjain (Madhya Pradesh).

Siva appears as time (Maha Kala).

The image of the God (Murti) shows his different 'qualities': on the banks of the Ganges at Rishikesh (Uttar Pradesh), there are votive statues of Vishnu and Lakshmi, of Durga and Krishna.

Next double page: A priest enters the temple of Vishnu at Shrirangam (Tamil Nadu). The colonnades of the marriage hall (kalyana maṅdapa) are decorated with horsemen trampling down beings that represent human passions.

'He who sees his Lord
In every creature
Dwelling for all eternity
Among mortals,
He perceives the truth.
He who sees separate lives
Of all the creatures here below
Reunited in the Brahman
Who bore them
Will himself find the Brahman.'

Bhagwad Gîtâ

◁ Birth of Durga in a column of flame (temple of Chidambaram, Tamil Nadu).

Columns of the temple of Siva Nataraja at Chidambaram (Tamil Nadu).

Three times a day, in order to awaken the gods and prompt them to visit the holy place, temple musicians play in front to the sanctuary (garbhagriha, embryo of the universe), in the heart of the building (temple of Siva at Tiruvanamalai, Tamil Nadu). Or else they may sing in the hall of prayer, to the accompaniment of the harmonium and the tabla, the epic poems, the *Purana*, or other religious texts (temple of Siva at *Somanatha*).

Before the offering of the worshipper is made, musicians effect three times and from left to right, the pradakshina—march around the sanctuary—to the beat of drums (chendar) in the temple of Ettumanuz (Kerala).

'In truth, the body of the god comes from his mental formula, from his verbal seed.' (Yamala Tantra). To be liberated, the priest will repeat three times, morning, noon and night, the mental formula of Vishnu: *Om! Namo Narayanaya.* The pujari (priest performing the puja) of the temple of Siva in Chidambaram makes his ritual exercises.

— Rubbing his temples, the priest invokes *Ganesha*.
— Beginning of the sandhya, the prayer every high caste Hindu must recite at the propitious hour.
— Vow to perform the ritual faithfully (sankalpa).
— Invocation to the sacred rivers (tarpana).
— Prayer to the ancestors (pravara).
— Control of breathing (pranayama).
— Offering of water (arghya).

The priest then raises his eyes to the sun in contemplation, shielding them with intertwined fingers and lets himself be filled with the cosmic energy. He recites the triple chant that protects vital energy.

'Om! Earthly sphere, spatial sphere, celestial sphere,
Let us look upon the might of the solar spirit, the divine
Creator. May he guide our spirits. Om!'

Agni—fire—is the mediator between man and gods. He may appear under his natural form or some ritual aspect. At the temple of Siva in Chamba (Himachal Pradesh), Agni appears under one of his ritual forms: he is the fire of the sacrifice by which the priest effects the rites of oblation and sanctifies the sanctuary.

Before honouring the god, the priest sanctifies all the other gods by fire. At the temple of Siva, at Chidambaram (Tamil Nadu), the priest makes an offering to Nandi. Occasionally, certain exceptional rituals may take place before the main ceremony. The offering of food represents the perception of the principle of immortality: the priest pours clarified butter (ghi) on to the fire. Temple of Raghunathji at Kulu (Himachal Pradesh).

On the feast day of Vishnu, in the temple of Varadaraja Swami in Kanchipuram, the god is ceremoniously carried around the temple on a palanquin preceded by the Brahmins of the temple; behind the procession, the *ganapaty* (religious leaders) chant the Vedic hymns.

Awakened with due solemnity, the god is ritually washed, dried, and clothed. The celebrant at the temple of Vishnu at Shrirangam decorates a statue of Krishna with jewels offered by the faithful, and freshly picked flowers, while incense and oil lamps are burned in his honour.

Pages 136 and 137:
'The gods came near the Great Goddess and asked: "Who are you?" She replied "I am the shape of Immensity. From me was born the world as Nature and Person."' *(Devi Bhagavata)*.

In the family sanctuary at Poomulli, Kerala, a priest renders homage to Devi (the Great Goddess); with his hands he makes the ritual tantric gestures (mudra) while reciting hymns of praise to the goddess of Devi Mahatmya.

134

The cult of Narsingh, the lion-man, is an ancient one. The priest of the family temple of Kachipuram (Tamil Nadu) hails the courage and the strength shown by this fourth incarnation of Vishnu. According to the prescribed ritual the priest moves fire before the altar; pours lustral water on the effigy; offers sacred food to the priests (prasad); offers fire; offers water.

Then follow the blessings, praise, adoration until all assembled partake of the holy food.

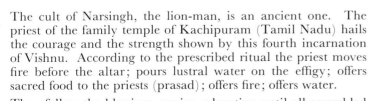

FESTIVALS

follow the gregorian calendar, but Hindu and Moslem festivals are calculated according to the lunar calendar, so the date changes every year.

Different groups of Hindus observe different new years. For the Gujaratis Diwali marks the eve of the new year. The Parsis celebrate Nauroz on 21 March, the same as in Iran. The Kashmiri Hindus' new year Naurey is the same as the Gudi Padwâ of Mahârâshtra, the Ugadhi of Karnâtaka and Ândhra. Everyone has a different type of celebration. The Punjâbis have Baisâkhî which falls on 13 April. Bengal and Assam observe their New Year which falls around the same time.

Every year in autumn, at the time of the full moon, the Rajputs gather to honour Brahma, the god of all creation, at the temple of Pushkar, near Ajmer.
Hundreds of thousand complete the pilgrimage, then come to the market. Along the dusty roads that lead to the holy place, camel-drivers lead the caravans to their encampment.

Covered with heavy jewelry, the young Rajput girls lift their veils for a quick glance at the proud shepherd who may carry them off. Perhaps they remember some desert legend, like the one of Dhola and Maru, two lovers who were reunited despite themselves by the artful wiles of a lame camel.

The market is the place to ride on the swings or to meet faraway relatives. At sundown, the animals are herded out amid loud bleatings and the ochre dust of the dunes. The last camel is whipped, the last orders shouted. Columns form and start off in the cool evening air. Camel drivers know the desert and travel along at an easy pace. Far beyond the dunes, before day breaks, they will have arrived at the next village.

Music and folkloric dances of India. Each region treasures its folklore: the feast days break the course of the year, bringing moments of gaiety to the country people as a change from the austere routine of their daily life.

The celebration of the feast of Dussehra at Kulu (Himachal Pradesh). It recalls, at the same time (according to the region) Rama's victory of his enemy Ravana, and the victory of Durga over the demon buffalo, Mahishasura; either way it is the defeat of Evil, symbolized by the brute force of a Demon. In the valley of Kulu, peasants follow the procession of local gods: to pull the heavy palanquin, covered with bright cloth, of the god Raghunathji (Lord of Raghu, a name of Rama) is considered a special blessing.

For many centuries, the epic of the *Ramayana* has been extraordinarily popular, as is shown by an immense effigy of Ravana, to be burnt at nightfall on the banks of the Ganges at Rishikesh, and the young child playing the part of Sîtâ, the wife of Rama, the symbol of married love.

When the mustard flowers in the fields, Northern India celebrates the feast of spring (Vasanta). At this time, the faithful worship Sarasvati, the goddess of learning and of the arts.

In the Gujarat, at the time of the feast of Holî that commemorates the love games of *Radha* and *Krishna*, villagers erect a clay statue that represents the demon lord *Hiranyakasipu*, defeated by Vishnu.

Preceded by two elephants and their parasols, emblems of sovereign- ▷
ty, pilgrims draw the heavy chariot of goddess Sarasvati through the streets of Sringeri (Mysore).

Skanda, the son of Siva and Parvati, is almost exclusively venerated in the Dravidian country today. *Muruga* and several old-time Southern gods have been united in him. In the villages, the men dance with frenzy, carrying on their shoulders the heavy kavadi (yokes) as a penance. Some say these dancers represent the warriors of *Muruga*'s army.

The Kerala is a land of strange beliefs. Of all of India, it is here that the pre-Aryan customs have best been preserved: the dance of Velisapad lets families know the wishes of the Great Goddess; the priest with his flashing sword is possessed by the very spirit of the Goddess.

North of Malabar, the feasts of Therayattam are held from January to March: masked dancers execute what seems to be a synthesis of all the different cults rendered to the Great Goddess and to the ancestors. From daybreak to dusk, the masked divinities dance without ceasing. The most popular of all is Kanda-karnan, who bears a towering structure of bamboo leaves over eighteen feet high and is surrounded by a ring of fire. The masks change from one village to the next. Here masked figures dance to the beat of the drums: underground forces appear, such as the earthquakes represented here by Kuttichatan.

Of the many masks of Therayattam, the most appreciated by the Malabar women is Ushitta, dressed in wide skirts of palm fronds, or else Chamunda, who represents the emanation of Durga the inaccessible, destroyer of demons.

The Kerala, land of the Malayali, is filled in spring with the sound of drums announcing village and temple feasts. At Ottapalam, dancers celebrating Devi wear huge head pieces of carved wood, or masks to honour Dravidian deities. To placate the spirits, the dances are all extremely violent. Villagers bearing huge reed horses covered with cloth prepare to joust for the entertainment of their audience. Gold-caparisoned elephants carry priests to a ceremony at the temple of Siva in Peringode.

The Puram, feast of the Sivite temples, is enthusiastically celebrated at Trichur in April or early May. This feast attracts millions of spectators to watch the celebrated procession of elephants in battle formation. Musicians play all day: beating their drums in frantic rhythm, clashing their cymbals or blowing their bugles.

Preceding double page: The regatta at Aranmulla.

Paipad regatta.

Once the harvest is in, the Malayali prepare the feast of Onam, whose main attraction is a boat
(vallomkali) race on rivers swollen by the monsoon. At Aranmulla, the long boats compete in speed on
the Pamba river where water jousts are held. Each boat, painted in the colours of its proprietor or
village, is manned by a hundred oarsmen, who chant in rhythm to speed up the beat of the paddles.

At Palni (Tamil Nadu), noted for its pilgrimage to *Muruga*, devotees endure painful mortifications.

Some pierce their skin with silver skewers. Another, hanging by hooks, offers holy ashes among the pilgrims. Others walk over hot embers.

PILGRIMAGES

The ancients understood the urgency of providing centripetal forces, and of establishing tenets deep within the racial unconscious that made possible a unitary feeling for the land and its contours. From the time of the Purânas, pilgrimage was regarded as a necessity for the regeneration of the spirit and the quickening of cultural exchange. Considered practically obligatory, pilgrimage became a milestone in man's life, when he left home and travelled the dusty paths to unknown lands. Holy sites were established at the cardinal points of the country—to the north were the snow-peaked highlands of Badrinâth, Kedârnâth and Amarnâth, to the east Puri, to the south Râmeshwaram and Kanyâkumârî, to the west Dwârka and in the centre, the heart, Kâshi or Vârânasî, Prayâg-Allâhâbad and Mathurâ.

Pilgrimage was an integrating of peoples and customs, and a sensing of the integral unity of the land. The ancient trade routes along which the pilgrim travelled were the same as taken from the very earliest times by the warrior, the adventurer, the trader, the jogi, the seeker and teacher of wisdom. The sage Agastya travelled along these routes to take the sacred Vedas and the Upanishads south of the Vindhyas. Vâlmîki, who wrote the Râmâyana nearly three thousand years ago, displays knowledge of the geophysical condition of the lands that lay along Râma's travels to Lankâ in search of Sîtâ. Perhaps he himself travelled along the same route to Lankâ. For centuries the Buddhist Bhikkus and the Jain munis trod these paths. Along them came Fahsien and Huen-tsang all the way from distant China eager to follow in the sacred footsteps of the Buddha.

Arts flourished at these sacred sites.

Important factors in our cultural integration were the Bauls, the jogis, the fakirs and the kathâ vâchaks or story-tellers. Travelling along these old paths they visited villages, festivals and places of pilgrimage. The stories of the Râmâyana and the Mâhâbhârata reached all parts of the country. Thus did the magnificent lyrical asthapadi of Jayadev's Geet Govind, written in Sanskrit in the twelfth century, travel to Assam, Orissa, Gujarat, Andhra and Kerala. The terse lyrical imagery of the verses have inspired painters, wood-carvers and sculptors.

India is a land of story. The early kathâs incorporated into the Purânas dealt with magic, song, social relationship, religious performance, heroic encounters and the loves of gods and men. Stories sung or spread by word of mouth, the art of the kathâ enriched the vernaculars. A vast number of stories on the sagacity of animals and birds appear in the 'Panchatantra' and the 'Jâkata' tales. Somadev's 'Kathâ Sarit Sâgar', or Ocean of Story, written in the eleventh century, is the earliest known compendium of these ancient tales. The original was claimed to have been written in an aboriginal language. In them Hindu mythology, Buddhist doctrine and Tântric ritual co-exist.

The white marble temples of Palitana, joined by a labyrinth of galleries, shelter the images of the twenty-four Thirthankara—or holy Jains: those who prepare the way. The temple of Ranakpur (Rajasthan) is proof of the profound
piety and riches of the Jain faithful.

In order to reach the residence of guru Dattatreya and of Ambaji, Durga, on the greatest height of the three summits of the Girnar pilgrimage, the devotee must climb some nine thousand steps. At the top he can adore the holy footprints and offer the sacred paesom on the way down to the monkeys from the nearby forest, just as Rama gave thanks to **Hanumân** for his help in freeing Sîtâ.

Over six hundred wide steps lead in zig-zags to the top of 'Kite hill'. Each morning pilgrims watch the darshana of two eagles: legend tells that these two white eagles are the reincarnations of two rishi who fly from Benares to this rock each morning to receive sacred rice from the Brahman.

Before making the pilgrimage to Sabarimalai, dedicated to the child-god Ayappan, the pilgrim will fast severely for forty days, dress in black and let beard and hair grow.

Kutiyur is the most ancient pilgrimage of Malabar: it takes place for thirty-four days at the beginning of the monsoon (July). In the heart of a deep jungle, that can be reached only at that time, Siva appears under his aspect as a destroyer, Rudra. White-robed pilgrims walk three times around the sanctuary surrounded by the river. Some go the whole way by rolling in the river bed. Only after this do they go up to the altar to honour the Siva linga.

At Bodh Gaya, the place where Siddharta practiced asceticism for six years, meditated and reached Supreme Knowledge, Buddhist monks (bhikshu) eat the food they have collected in their wooden begging bowls (patta).

Almost each town has a mosque (masjid). The mosque of Siddi Sayyid in Ahmedadad has particularly fine decorations.

In Kerala, the first Syrian Christians were joined by Hindus converted to catholicism by Portuguese and French missionaries in the sixteenth century. On the feast of St Thomas who, according to legend, evangelized the area, relics and statues of the holy apostles are brought out in procession.

Thousands of pilgrims climb the narrow path that leads to Amarnath.
To die on the way is a blessing given by the Almighty.

In August, in Pahalgam (Kashmir) a silver stick, symbolizing Siva, opens the procession of the pilgrimage to Amarnath, and is preceded by singers to proclaim the glory of the 'Great Lord'.

Pages 190 and 191: At Panchtarni, the place where five rivers meet, the pilgrims' encampment recalls the camps of the caravans that once crossed the Himalayas.

Fervently, the pilgrims cross the highest pass, at 4800 meters, that will lead them to the grotto. Legend says that Parvati, wanting to know the secret of immortality, asked Siva to reveal it. Parvati was led far into the mountain, where Siva spoke of the Truth. Parvati fell asleep. The Lord heard a noise and looking up saw two birds twittering their thanks. Since then, there are always two birds in the sky of Amarnath. In the cavern, pilgrims worship a stalagmite as the linga of Siva.

The great poet *Kâlidas* made a graceful description of the meeting of Ganga and Jamuna at Prayag. He compared it to matching a necklace of sapphires with another of pearls, a garland of white lotus to another of blue lilies.

The Maha Kumbha Melâ: From all parts of India, millions of pilgrims throng, once every twelve years, to Prayâg, named Allâhâbâd by Emperor Akbar, at Triveni Sangam, where the Ganges, the Jamuna and the mythical river Sarasvati all join.

At the propitious moment (muhurta) at four o'clock in the morning, believers say that those who bathe in the sangam attain immortality. In long processions, the sadhu come down from the Himalayas lead the human flood to sanctify themselves at the meeting-place (sangam) of the three rivers.

Page 199: During the Melâ, popular theatre groups give scenes from Hindu mythology. A child plays the part of Krishna.

The Sikhs are distinguished by the beard, long hair knotted at the top of the head and covered by large turbans (pheta), an iron bracelet and the kirpani or dagger, at the side. Followers of guru *Nanak*, they recognize the truth of other religions and take part in the Kumbha Melâ.

Religious characters, 'holy men' mingle with the effigies of the gods. The crowd reveres an image of Krishna, on a dais under an awning.

The wise men are the centre, the heart of the Kumbha Melâ. The faithful flock to hear the teachings of these venerated people. For hours, the masses await the appearance of the sage they call Baba: hundreds of palms are outstretched to catch the grain that has been consecrated by the old sage, said to be a 114 years old.

Pilgrimages to the sources of the Ganges: Hardvar is the starting point for the pilgrimages into the Himalayas. This city is the door to the holy places of Kedarnath, Badrinath, Yamnotri and Gangotri. At Har-ki-Pauri, pilgrims worship the Gangâ as a holy Mother whose waters cleanse them from ill. At sunrise, devotees watch the ceremony of Arti, or offering of fire. Top left: Gangâ, garlanded in flowers.

Pages 208 and 209: The site of Kedarnath (Uttar Pradesh), at the foot of the Himalayas.

'...The Ganges falls from the sky on to the head of Siva, from the head of Siva on to the Himalayas, from high in the Himalayas on to the earth, from the earth into the ocean, and thence into the lower regions: those who no longer believe, disappear in the same way through a hundred issues...'

A pilgrim, on the banks of the Ganges, offers food to the ravens, the messengers of Yama, god of Death. At the joining of the rivers, Alaknandâ and Rishi Gangâ, stands the temple of Badrinath. The *Skanda Purana* tells that *Adiguru*, while climbing a mountain to reach a place called Ashta Kund in order to meditate, was told by a wise man that he should put back in its place an image of Vishnu that had fallen into the depths of the Narad Kund. Diving in, *Adiguru* found the idol and set it up again.

From the Kalind Parvat flows the Jamuna. The sage Asit used to bathe each day in the waters of the Jamuna and the Ganges. When he became old and could no longer go to Gangotri, a new spring gushed forth symbolizing Gangâ. In this sacred spot, a holy man is always seated, even in the cold of winter.

PATHS
OF
WISDOM

Among the great discoverers of the paths of wisdom as we know them through the Vedas and Upanishads were Angirasa Rishis, perhaps the most ancient ones. Later we have the illumined leaders such as Vasishtha, Vishwâmitra, Lopâmudrâ and Agastya. Many other illustrious ones have also been named in the epics. And then we come to the next cycle, a new era.

The heroic probers into the unknown were the first intellectuals and thinkers, men who broke the accepted bondages of thought and tradition.

Buddha, Mahâvîra, Kapila were the great teachers of this era. Denying the rigidity which vested interests create over a period of time, they enlarged the horizons of the human mind and of man's relationship to life and the cosmos.

From the teachings of the Buddha and Mahâvîra were born the feeling of sanctity for all human life and the basic urge to freedom from violence to all living things.

Buddha left home, family, wealth to seek answers to the fundamental problems of man: sickness, old age and death, to sorrow and freedom from sorrow. He preached the illumined teaching of the Dharma at Sârnâth in the holy city of Kâshi. His words were like rain to parched soil. To the cosmic perceptions of the Upanishad teachings was added a new dimension, that of Karunâ, compassion.

The Buddha preached self-reliance and equality. He said, 'Rouse thyself by thyself, examine thyself by thyself, thus self protected and attentive will thou live happily, O bikkhu.' And again, 'Go unto all lands and preach this gospel, tell them, the poor and the lowly, the rich and the high and all castes, to unite in this religion as do all rivers in the sea.'

Buddha's communion with nature, his tentative and gentle approach to life and wish to live without causing injury to the earth, to plant, animal and man is expressed in this beautiful simile. 'As the bee collects nectar and departs without injuring the flower or its colour or scent, so let a sage dwell in his village.'

In the following centuries, the teachings of the Buddha exploded all over India and were taken by Buddhist monks to distant parts of Asia. Kumârajiva and Bodhidharma endured severe hardships to carry the words of the Enlightened One to China, from where the teaching spread to Japan. Padmasambhava journeyed to Tibet to preach and practise.

The words of the Buddha were taken across the seas to what is now Indonesia, Malaysia, Thailand and Vietnam. Wherever Buddhism spread, there was a germination of new life. A monumental art, quickened and transformed by the nature of silence and compassion, evolved, giving sensitivity to the sculptured form of animal, bird or man. Great universities and centres of learning were established at Taxilâ, Nâlandâ, and Vikramsilâ, attracting scholars from all parts of the world. They brought with them a way of life and thought, contributing to the maturing of this country's culture, and took back with them the riches of mind and perceptive knowledge that was this country's heritage.

The common man regarded Buddhism not as a separate religion, but as one of the ways to salvation. In time, Buddhism was wholly absorbed into the Vedantic creed and Buddha was recognised as an incarnation of Vishnu. In the land of his birth the adoration remained, but the teaching disappeared. In recent years there has been a revival.

214

Among the great teachers of the breakaway tradition, was Mahâvîra. It is astonishing that he lived and taught in the same part of the country and at the same time as the Buddha and founded the religion of the Jains (the conquerors). Like the Buddha, Mahâvîra too was born of a ruling family. At thirty he left home and family to become an ascetic. He taught freedom from the bondage of Karma through a life of extreme rigid discipline in which a limitation of wants and desires was fundamental. His reverence for life was absolute and all-pervasive. From this sprang the doctrine of non-violence which has contributed so much to our struggle for freedom. Mahâvîra's disciples walked the length and breadth of India to spread his teachings. Many temples and centres of learning were established and survive to this day. The colossal rock-cut image of Gomateshwara in Karnâtaka will be a thousand years old in 1981. Jainism remained a living religion. Its impact on the rest of the world has been minimal.

By the eighth century A.D., Shankarâchârya, one of India's youngest and greatest religious teachers, travelled from the South to the Himalayas. He met philosophers and dialecticians, reasoned and convinced, and conveyed his tremendous passion and perceptions to the thinkers of the age. A brilliant philosopher-saint, he preached the doctrine of the Vedânta, based on the Upanishads—the world was maya or illusion, the ultimate reality was 'Brahman', to be revealed in the stillness of meditation. His doctrine came to be known as the Advaita (Non-Dual) doctrine.

Shankarâchârya was a great organiser and established an order of monks and four main monasteries at the cardinal points of the land at Sringeri in Karnâtaka, Dwârkâ in Gujarat, Badrînâth in Uttar Pradesh and Purî in Orissa. They still thrive, as does a living order of Shankarâchârya's monks.

Saint Thiruvalluvar (first or second century) was the oldest regional poet of India whose aphorisms on morals, virtue, love and happiness have become a part of the idiom of the Tamil language, such as 'learned fools are they who cannot move in harmony with the world.' His book 'Kural' is called the 'Veda in miniature', 'the mustard seed in which is comprehended the riches of the seven seas'.

Basava (twelfth century A.D.), a Saivaite saint of South India, was a religious teacher, social reformer and revolutionary who opposed image worship, rejected the Vedas and the authority of the priests and instituted complete equality among his followers, and even equality for women. He was the founder of the Lingayat sect.

In the early centuries, religious persecution in other countries compelled all those who suffered to escape for security, and many landed on our shores. Historical records show that missionaries who had accompanied traders from distant lands, remained here to preach and to build their own places of worship. Many of these small religious communities survive and flourish as separate identifiable sects and have made their mark in national affairs.

A South Indian tradition maintains that St Thomas, one of the first disciples of Jesus Christ and an architect by profession, was invited from Syria by King Gondophernes to help to build his capital. St Thomas remained to teach, preach and convert people to his faith. Legend to this day indicates a site at Mylapore in Madras as his tomb.

The early Christians were Nestorians. Their missionaries established the Christian Church of South India. Later, the advent of Islam in the West Asian countries compelled Christians to come from Syria and settle in Malabar. A thriving Syrian Christian community around Cochin bears witness to this. Thus we see that Christianity came to India long before it was accepted by Europe.

There is a legend that Christ visited Kashmir during the years when little is known of His whereabouts. Another claims that He actually died near Srînagar where a tomb-stone with such an inscription was said to have been found.

The Jewish faith in Malabar has existed for nearly 2,000 years with never an incident of persecution or discrimination. The synagogue in Cochin celebrated its 400th anniversary some years ago.

A picturesque story illustrates the typical Indian attitude to religious immigrants. About 1,300 boat loads of Zoroastrian fire-worshippers from Persia landed on the West coast of India. The Hindu king welcomed their leader to the court to ask what they wanted. There being no common language they had to speak in signs. The leader of the Zoroastrians called for a pitcherful of water and dropped a coin into it—to signify that his group would live quietly without disturbing the rest of society. The king asked for a jug of milk to be brought and poured a spoonful of sugar into it: it was his way of assuring the newcomers that they were welcome to live in his kingdom. He followed this up by issuing an edict that the Zoroastrians would be allowed to practise their religion and keep their customs, but must adopt the local dress and language so as not be too conspicuously different and be able to live in harmony. Ten centuries have passed, their descendants, known as Pârsis, have prospered in India. Although the community is less than a hundred thousand in number, the Pârsis have risen to the top in many professions, notably in industry and in politics. They have kept intact their religion and their rituals. Some local influences have crept in. The Pârsis present an example of India's very special kind of assimilation without obliteration of distinctive diversity.

Islam was brought to this country by Arab traders and fakirs long before the Moslem invasions of the North. Like some other founders of religions, Mohammad was a rebel against many existing social customs. His simple and direct preaching, coupled with the flavour of democracy, attracted the masses in neighbouring countries. Indeed its message of equality and self-help had a tremendous appeal for the oppressed everywhere. Islam means perfect tranquility or to surrender oneself to Him with whom peace is made. The Quran says, 'It is your own conduct which will lead you to paradise or hell.'

There were Moslem invasions from the North and more Moslem dynasties arose in Delhi and other parts of the country, but all of them regarded India as their home. Attracted by royal patronage, Moslem soldiers and divines came from other parts of the Islamic world. But holy men like Moiuddin Chisti of Ajmer, Nizâmuddin Aulia of Delhi and Baba Farid came to be regarded first and foremost as Indian saints. There was powerful interaction of Hindu and Islamic philosophical ideas and Moslem poets of India have given expression to it through the centuries—whether it be Amir Khusrau of the fourteenth century or Mohammad Iqbal of the twentieth.

Sufism was a mixture of Islam and Vedânta. The Sufi mystic saints, together with Hindu saints formed a fraternity.

In the Middle Ages, Kabir was brought up in the humble home of a Moslem weaver of Vârânasî, on the banks of the Gangâ. Through poetry resonant with the nuances of the local vernacular, rich in imagery and symbol, he taught a mystical doctrine visualising God beyond caste or creed, beyond the confines of Hinduism or Islam. His poetry continues to form part of the language of Moslem and Hindu alike. All communities claim him.

Hindus and Moslems worship at each others' shrines. There are Moslem priests at some Hindu shrines, such as Bidbhanjan temple of Hanumân in Gujarat and the Amarnâth shrine in Kashmir. The Darga Sharif of Ajmer in Rajasthan is known as the Mecca of India and attracts large numbers of Moslems as well as Hindus.

Of course, there were conflicts between liberal cosmopolitans and the orthodox. Some Sultans pursued conversion through the sword, more often for reasons of State than to gain religious merit. Other rulers were totally free from fanaticism. The best example was Akbar the Great, under whom the **Moghul** empire reached its zenith in the sixteenth century. Akbar was a conscious synthesiser, who even sought to promulgate a new syncretic religion. But for centuries before him, Moslem and Hindu ideas had interacted to produce a new amalgam in art and architecture in music and language. Moslem musicians sang of Krishna and Hindus of Allah with the same lyrical adoration. The Urdu language is a living speech born out of this synthesis.

The Sikhs are a virile people. The largest number live in Punjab, but they are spread all over the country and indeed in the farthest parts of the globe.

Philosophers and saints such as Chaitanya and others of the fifteenth and sixteenth centuries belong to the stage of development where the concern was not only with the inner mind, but to touch man's whole being and activity. There was also during this period a remarkable attempt to combine Vedânta and Islam to establish a more lasting communal harmony. In particular the work of Guru Nanak and of the subsequent Sikh Khalsa movement was astonishingly original and novel. In no sense was this a revivalism. It was an outburst of fresh creativity, based on an assimilation of the past. Nanak said, 'Truth is high but higher still is truthful living.'

However, the time was not ripe then and it was only in the nineteenth century that the seed germinated into a new spiritual impulse. Great pioneers and reformers appeared.

Swâmi Dayânanda Saraswatî founded the Ârya Samâj, perhaps to curb the influence of Islam and Christianity. Thus there was a certain militancy in the movement. Conversion which had so far not been known to Hinduism was now introduced. A good deal of work was done by members of this organisation for education and to improve the living conditions of the weaker sections and backward classes.

Many were influenced by various aspects of western liberal thought. Through their work the entire country was electrified, not only spiritually but even socially and politically. Nationalism came to be proclaimed as the new spirituality and from the beginning was international in its spirit and sweep.

Râjâh Râm Mohan Roy was a scholar with a truly scientific mind. He founded the Brâhmo Samâj movement which was confined to the educated and westernized middle classes, mostly of Bengal. Above all, he was a reformer.

Born in Kerala in the late nineteenth century, Nârâyana Guru was an Ezhava, one of the most under-privileged of groups. He made it his mission to break caste barriers and preached of 'one caste, one religion, one God'. He became known as the 'Guru whose breath is hope and whose touch is life'.

A wonderful man, Râmakrishna Paramhansa, was what we in India consider an enlightened soul, a person who 'knew' and 'was', without having to learn or make any effort. He practised the sadhana (spiritual practice) of every religion. He inspired many to service. Even those who considered themselves rationalists were impressed by his spiritualism and radiance. Most notable amongst his disciples was the shining figure of Vivekânanda whose faith and intense love of country made him an ideal interpreter of our philosophy. He was aware of our weaknesses and did not hesitate to chide and urge Indians to break away from apathy and lethargy, and superstitious customs.

In Râmakrishna's name was founded the non-sectarian mission which has an unbroken and unblemished record of service, especially in the fields of health and education.

The problem of man was viewed in the context of his future evolution and also as an interaction between matter and spirit. Sri Aurobindo, intensely patriotic and a revolutionary, described by Romain Rolland as 'the completest synthesis of the East and the West', declared man to be a transitional being who needed to undergo an integral spiritual transformation, not by escaping to some far heaven but here and now on this physical earth. This he felt was an issue of the whole world's upward expectation and fulfilment.

The Mother (Madame Mirra Alfassa) came from France in 1914 to meet Sri Aurobindo and made India her permanent home to collaborate with him and to fulfil the task of integral transformation. She attained the highest spirituality and the near future will show the revolutionary effects of her work for humanity, for its lasting unity and harmony, and for its transmutation into superhumanity.

We have no dearth of modern-day sages or 'gurus', as they are more commonly known. Some perform miracles, some are in communication with God and others have no hesitation in claiming godhood for themselves. No doubt each has something to offer which satisfies the needs felt by his disciples. Many of these gurus have large foreign followings and ashrams abroad. If people find solace in them, who are we to demur? *Honi soit qui mal y pense!* This great and rather sudden demand for gurus, this ready and what seems to be unquestioning acceptance, is it not an indication of a restlessness, an emptiness of spirit? And where but within oneself can one find rest? And where but within oneself can one find fulfilment? Kabir has written, 'I laugh when I hear that the fish in the water is thirsty. You do not see that the God is in your home. Go where you will, to Banâras or to Mathurâ, If you do not find your soul, the world is unreal to you.'

Yet the old tradition of the anonymous holy man does exist, not only on far off mountain-tops or in caves tucked away on the plains but even in the midst of the bustle of city life.

Such an enlightened person was Ramana Maharshi whose very presence moulded the thinking of many Indians and others who had the privilege of meeting him and listening to him.

A sage who attracts many, especially intellectuals and highly cultivated people, is the present Shankarâchârya of Kâncheepuram. One cannot but be moved to the core of one's being by the compassion on his countenance. The more quiet and the more still he is, the more potent is the vibration which emanates from him.

Jiddu Krishnamurti was chosen by Dr Annie Besant to be the World Teacher. He walked out of the vast organisation with its wealth and following. For he felt that truth cannot be institutionalised and that such organisations smother all religious enquiry. Man must be free to question. This freedom does not mean the licence to do what he wants but a state of mind that is free of all self-pursuits. Krishnamurti feels, in line with many of our great thinkers, that the world and society can change only when there is a fundamental revolution in the depths of man's mind and heart. He denies authority, gurus and disciplined beliefs, and all isms as barriers to self-knowing.

Mother Teresa, winner of the Nobel prize, now an Indian citizen, was born of Albanian parents in Yugoslavia. She has made a special place for herself, symbolising the very spirit of service and love. She works amongst those whom Tagore called 'the poorest, and lowliest, and lost'. Her base is India but her work spans the continents.

Vinoba Bhave, an erudite scholar in the literature of all the major religions, a writer and linguist, was chosen by Gandhi as the first volunteer to offer himself for arrest. Later, Gandhi declared him to be his spiritual heir as he had made Jawaharlal Nehru his political heir. Bhave devoted himself to Gandhi's village welfare programme, making a significant and original contribution of his own by starting the Bhoodan—donation of land—movement. He covered 80,000 kilometers on foot receiving 4 million acres and thus creating a psychological climate for the redistribution of land to the landless. This concept was further expanded to gramdan—voluntary surrender of land ownership rights—to the entire village community in an effort to help the 'last man'. Supporting Gandhi's belief that no mass programme could succeed without the enthusiastic participation of women, Vinoba Bhave stressed Stree Shakti—Woman Power. He speaks continuously of the need to temper science with spirituality as the only way to ensure the proper use of science for the benefit of mankind.

Sri Ânandmayî Mâ, as her name implies, seems truly to embody bliss. In the world but not of it, she is a typical example of pure devotion.

Philosophy, saints and gurus can give guidance but ultimately each human being stands alone and must depend on his own inner resources. This is what the Buddha meant when he gave his parting advice, 'Be a light unto yourself, be a refuge unto yourself.'

The Jagatguru of Kanchipuram (Tamil Nadu) receives the homage of his devotees. The 'universal master' is considered a high spiritual authority; he heads one of the four monasteries founded by the philosopher *Shankaracharya* in the seventh century.

The faithful, gathered around ▷ the image of Krishna, chant the glorious name of Ram to the accompaniment of cymbals and tambourines (Modhera, Gujarat).

◁ Draped in a shawl inscribed with the name of Ram, a woman meditates on the steps leading to the Ganges, in Benares.

At Udayapur, pilgrims come to pray before the statue of Mirabai, the mystic princess who gave up wordly possessions to sing the love of Krishna.

Ananda Mayi Ma blesses her visitors in her ashram at Benares. She is one of the most venerated spiritual teachers of India.

On the steps of the temple of Palni (north east of Madurai, Tamil Nadu), a little boy plays the part of Balakrishna, the child god.

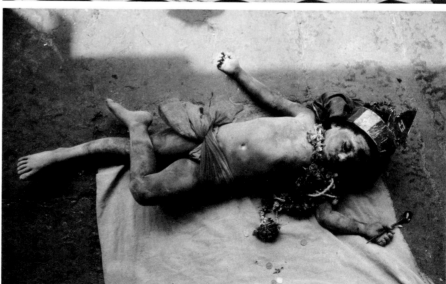

In the courtyard of the temple of Ramdeogarh, in Rajasthan, a man practices asceticism by reading the sacred texts (jnana yoga, or the way of learning).

'The birds come fearlessly near the blessed who live in mountain caves, contemplating the supreme light, and drink the tears of happiness that pour from their eyes...'

Giving up their families, their caste and the world, nothing will turn these searchers after truth away from their search for the divine. They are called sannyasi (those who renounce all).

Brahmins meditate on the sacred writings.

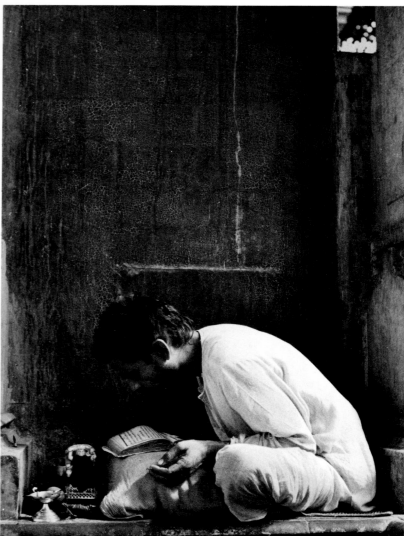

At Ujjain, in the very grotto where *Bhartrihari* meditated, there is always a Sivite hermit.

A traditional guru receives the offerings of his disciples at Tiruvayur (Tamil Nadu).

RENUNCIATION
AND ENLIGHTENMENT

A jogi at Agastya Malai (Tamil Nadu). It is here that the wise man *Agastya* made penance to maintain the earth's equilibrium at the time of the wedding of Siva and Parvati: since all the gods had gathered at the top of Mount Kailasa, they almost threw the world out of balance.

A sadhu makes the offering of a lotus blossom to Siva Linga, at the grotto of Nilakantha (a name given to Siva meaning the blue-throated God) in Mandu.
'One God alone: Siva or Vishnu.
One friend alone: a prince or a hermit.
One home alone: a town or a forest.
One wife alone: the beloved or a cave in the mountains.'

(Verses of Bharthrihari).

An offering to Siva linga in the grotto of Pachmari (Madhya Pradesh).
In the back of the cave, likenesses of Siva, Vishnu and Brahma.

Covered in ashes an ascetic meditates in the middle of a circle of fire.
A sadhu blows a conch horn during morning prayer.

Jain hermits come out of their retreat to prostrate themselves before the statue of a Thirthankar at Kalugunalai.

A hermit returns to his sanctuary in Agastya Malai.

Acharya Nirvan Swami, a holy Jain in meditation at Kalugumalai. Behind him are the rock carvings of Thirthankara.

An ascetic, in the Himalayas, makes offerings of water and jasmine blossoms to the Ganges.

'As the waters of the Ganges and the Jamuna are mingled, so are mingled in the heart of the pious searcher after truth, the currents of life and sacrifice. In his heart, the sacred waters flow day and night, and thus ends the cycle of births and deaths...'

INDIA TODAY

India's reputation for wealth—the precious stones and ivory, the spices and rich textiles, the skill of its artisans—was bound to attract invaders. Many came to plunder and loot. But almost all remained to be absorbed and to add something new to our composite culture, our Indianness. The founders of the Moslem dynasties came from outside, but they became Indians, employing Hindus at their courts. The Hindu kingdoms which existed side by side also employed Moslem generals and administrators. A notable case is of Akbar marrying Jodhabai, a Rajput Princess, and the charming though tragic love story of Baz Bahadur and his beautiful Hindu wife Rupmati. Like Fatehpur Sikri, Akbar's abandoned city near Agra, Baz Bahadur's Mandu in Central India has preserved the atmosphere of those times and one has the impression that the inhabitants have just moved out. Akbar employed Hindus in many strategic posts.

A fine embodiment of this spirit was Shivaji (seventeenth century). While fighting against Aurangzeb, Akbar's bigoted descendant, he did not hesitate to employ Moslems in his army and navy. Out of people disunited, enfeebled by petty quarrels, he made a victorious army and a proud nation. Many contemporary occidental observers, particularly French, expressed their admiration for his gifts as an able general and liberal administrator. His best contemporary assessment comes from Barthelemy Carre who wrote in his *Voyage des Indes Orientales*: 'One of the greatest men the East has ever seen. In courage, the rapidity of his conquests and his great qualities, he does not ill resemble that great king of Sweden, Gustavus Adolphus. To this quickness of movement he added like Julius Caesar a clemency and bounty that won him the hearts of those his arms had worsted.'

The European conqueror was altogether different. He came to trade but could not resist the temptation of conquest which would yield far greater profit. This he did by force of arms, by bribery, by betrayal. Yet the blame is equally ours, for had the Indian rulers of the day not been weak and divided, had we not lost the capacity of creative thought, had we kept abreast of the technical advances of the West, we would not have so quietly, so cheaply fallen prey to the blandishments and assaults of foreigners.

Colonialism brought the disruption of our village industry, it upset traditional balances and division of labour. A new rich land-owning class was created of those who helped the new rulers. How can imperialism survive without oppression, humiliation and degradation? It completely impoverished a land renowned for its riches. Industry and agriculture were neglected, there was woeful absence of social services. All kinds of vested interests grew and new problems arose, such as those of the princes and the minorities.

In 1857, there was an uprising. The West called it a mutiny but we believe it to be much more a planned revolt. Unfortunately, premature action in one place put the Indians at a disadvantage. The ageing emperor of Delhi, Bahadur Shah Zafar, was made the symbol of resistance, but the actual battles were waged by rulers such as Peshwâ, the Rânî of Jhânsi, the Nawâb of Avadh and others. They fought valiantly but many were betrayed from within their own ranks. Also, the British had far superior weapons. But as a whole the Indian princes took the side of the British or waited to see who would win, as they still tend to do. Of the princes at that time, Thompson says, 'The Butler Committee (1928-29), appointed by the British Government to consider the problem of the Indian States, said in its report: "It is not in accordance with historical facts that when the Indian States (under the rule of the Maharajas) came into contact with the British power they were independent. Some were rescued, other were created by the British.'''

It would be wrong to think that Britain gave democracy to India. The Marquis of Zetland has this to say about the early Buddhist Assemblies: 'And it may come as a surprise to many to learn that in the Assemblies of the Buddhists in India 2,000 or more years ago are to be found the rudiments of our own parliamentary practice of the present day. The dignity of the Assembly was preserved by the appointment of a special officer, the embryo of Mr Speaker in the House of Commons. A second officer was appointed whose duty it was to see that when necessary a quorum was secured— the prototype of the parliamentary chief whip in our own system. A member initiating business did so in the form of a motion which was then open to discussion. In some cases this was done once only, in others three times, thus anticipating the practice of parliament in requiring that a Bill be read a third time before it became law. If discussion disclosed a difference of opinion the matter was decided by the vote of the majority, the voting being by ballot.' Elected Village Councils in India functioned fairly democratically until their powers were so reduced as to render them ineffective.

While the close contact with the West brought some fresh air, the colonisers obstructed the very change and progress which, in the larger context, they represented. They encouraged and consolidated the position of the socially reactionary groups in India, and opposed all those who worked for political and social change.

Long before Churchill declared in 1942 that the Atlantic charter did not apply to India, Indians were aware that the political principles which the British followed at home were meant only for the people of the sceptred isle and not for them. However, it is only fair to remember that these attitudes deeply troubled the conscience of a minority of non-conformists. Europe's enlightenment could not be confined to that continent. Many pioneering Indians were inspired by it to reform the wrongs of Indian society and to claim a place in the sun for their nation.

I never cease to wonder at the number of luminous personalities which India produced during that dark period of colonial rule, saints, reformers and revolutionaries who were deeply immersed in spirituality. Men and women of high intellect and capacity, each shone with his own light, each in his own way prepared the ground for the future renaissance.

Gandhi is known as the father of the nation. Each person's understanding of Gandhi is a measure of his own development. Not for decades will we be able to wholly gauge the extent of his work. He transformed the cowed and the meek into a nation which fearlessly asserted its right to be free. He brought changes on the political scene, but what is even more significant is his influence on the inner lives of people. He altered the sociological climate, breaking down the walls of discrimination. He was completely committed to non-violence and to peaceful methods, considering the means to be as important as the ends.

All religions have spoken of truth and peace, but it was Gandhi's genius to use these as tools in our struggle for Independence, which was waged through a mass movment of peaceful, non-violent non-cooperation. It was Gandhi's genius to have a correct assessment of the mood of the people and to give voice and direction to something which had been germinating beneath the surface for some time.

Mahatma Gandhi and others see no contradiction between the emphasis on non-violence and Krishna's advice in the Gîtâ to Arjuna to wage war. As Nehru explains it, 'Evidently, the conception of Ahinsa, non-violence, had a great deal to do with the motive, the absence of the violent mental approach, self-discipline and control of anger and hatred, rather than the physical abstention from violent action, when this became necessary and inevitable.'

Even during the struggle for Independence, we were deeply conscious that freedom did not mean merely the ending of foreign rule but a rebirth of our nation, the ending of poverty and inequality, of superstition and every kind of narrowness of spirit and thought. Hence the stress on Swadeshi or Indian goods and Khadi, the handspun and handwoven cloth we were all pledged to wear. It served as a uniform and at the same time gave employment and self-reliance to the peasant. Gandhi's leadership transformed the Indian National Congress from an elitist body to a mass movement whose programme of civil disobedience entailed much suffering and sacrifice. To go to prison in the cause of the nation became a point of honour.

It is customary to regard Gandhi as a typical Indian. A political and spiritual figure of his quality of course could not have been born in any other country. He revivified some of the oldest instincts and insights of Indian culture. He spoke the Indian idiom. Yet it would not be wise to ignore the Western influence on Gandhi or his own contemporaneity. He was not born with the loin-cloth. He acquired it after years of wearing Western apparel. He was deeply impressed by the West, more particularly, proselytising protestant England, and this experience made him in some ways more of an Indian and also more of a world citizen. Einstein remarked: 'Generations to come will scarcely believe that such a one as this, ever in flesh and blood, walked upon this earth.' But the world's recognition of Gandhi's greatness was belated. Now his ideas are attracting greater attention. Gandhi, Rabindranath Tagore, Motilal Nehru, Sarojini Naidu, Maulana Azad and Jawaharlal Nehru are to me outstanding examples of the fusion of East and West.

Gandhi designated Nehru as his heir because of his conviction that Nehru understood his fundamental principles and would act in that spirit, and also because there was no doubt that he was the people's choice. Nehru loved the Indian people and was proud of his Indian heritage. Once he wrote, 'If any people choose to think of me then I should like them to say: this was a man who with all his mind and heart loved India and the Indian people and they in turn were indulgent to him and gave him all their love most abundantly and extravagantly.'

Yet he was universal in spirit and his mind and heart encompassed the whole world. One Prime Minister of Britain called Jawaharlal Nehru the first citizen of the modern world and another, Sir Winston Churchill, described him as a man who had conquered hatred and fear. Nehru was a gracious, generous and vital human being who commanded an international audience reaching far beyond governments. He spoke for sensitive thinking men and women everywhere. Amongst his personal friends, he counted some of the best minds of his time—in science, arts and literature no less than in politics. Yet he was equally at home with the simplest peasant. He laid the foundation of modern India and built the infrastructure for progress in science and technology, for agriculture and for industry. He did not neglect any facet of national development in the social, economic or cultural spheres. He was anxious that we should not be alienated from our roots. His unequivocal espousement of certain principles and policies gave India a position and influence in world affairs much greater than her economic or military power (or lack of it) entitled her to. Not for a moment did he stray from Gandhi's ideals of dedicated service to the poor, of working towards giving equality of opportunity to all citizens and of not harming even those who harmed him.

Next to Gandhi, Nehru was greatly influenced by his father, Motilal Nehru, Tagore and Maulana Azad. Nehru's father Motilal was one of those grand personalities who always seem larger than life. A brilliant and self-made man who earned hugely and spent with equal lavishness, he enjoyed the good life but threw it overboard without a sigh or backward glance when his son Jawaharlal decided to follow Gandhi.

From every State arose leaders and many were of all-India stature, who would have made a mark in any country. Each district had its heroes and martyrs.

Maulana Azad was an arresting figure, learned and scholarly, a perfect example of India's composite culture. It was a delight to hear him talk, so apt, so precise and picturesque were his phrases. A sincere patriot and devout Moslem, he had deep respect for India's many-sidedness and brought balance and elegance to public life. He wrote: 'The Eastern conception of man's status, if combined with the Western concept of progress, would open out to man the possibility of infinite advance without the risk implied in the use of science.'

Not all were attracted by Gandhi's idealistic (but also obviously practical in our circumstances) approach. There were terrorist groups and violent outbreaks. There was a mutiny in the Indian Navy. All these played their part and we do recognise them as important contributions to our freedom movement. The martyrdom of several intrepid young persons thrilled the younger generation especially. But still they were on the periphery, apart from the great mass upsurge which shook the country and eventually the British Empire, and enveloped all of India in its sweep. Subhash Chandra Bose or Netaji as he is fondly called, was in a class by himself. Because of our strong feelings against fascism and Nazism, we could not approve of any kind of alliance with Hitler's Germany or Japan. Yet Subhash Chandra Bose's patriotism was never in doubt. He acted in all sincerity. The manner of his escape, his ingenuity and daring, and the setting up of the Indian National Army with its women's wing excited admiration. Later, when three Indian National Army men were to be court-martialled in Delhi's Red Fort, Jawaharlal Nehru took the lead in their defence. Netaji's 'Jai Hind' was adopted as our national slogan.

After Independence we faced a task of gigantic proportions, and in what circumstances! The partition of the country brought much human agony and inflicted wounds that have not healed. Hundreds of thousands of families were divided. Decades later, in wars between the two countries, brothers, uncles and other relations would find one another in opposing armies. In the thick of battle, a voice would reach across the lines to ask news of a village or a friend. We had to resettle the seemingly endless stream of refugees, so full of bitterness and revenge as they were, to rebuild an administration so sharply and suddenly reduced—even the chairs, typewriters, etc. being divided according to certain agreed formulas—while taking the first groping measures towards building a firm foundation for the modernisation that was to come.

The second stunning tragedy which rocked the nation was the assassination of our beloved leader, Mahatma Gandhi, father of the nation. 'The light has gone out of our lives,' said Nehru. But life has to go on and the nation's confidence in itself and its future upheld, and he was quick enough to add, 'Yet I was wrong. The light that has illumined this country for these many many years will illumine this country for many more years, and a thousand years later, that light will still be seen in this country, and the world will see it and it will give solace to innumerable hearts.' Perhaps it was the severity of these shocks that gave India the resilience to face all that followed in later years.

The first priority was to provide their basic needs to one-sixth of mankind within a generation or two, in conditions complicated by the competition and the constant pulling down by opposition parties, that is democracy. There was no data, no guidance. Had such a task been attempted ever in history? Planning and action, improvement of data leading to better planning and better action, all this was a continuous and overlapping process. We have learned by trial and error. Old problems continue and new ones constantly crop up. But one thought has grown, permeating all spheres, that we should re-order priorities and move away from the single-dimensional model which has viewed growth from certain limited angles and which seems to have given a higher place to things rather than people. We should have a more comprehensive approach to life, centred on man not as a statistic but as an individual with many sides to his personality. The solution of these problems cannot be isolated phenomena of marginal importance, but must be an integral part of the unfolding of the very process of development.

There is no conflict between industrial development and rural development. On the contrary, each complements the other. Periods of drought and agricultural stagnation have deeply affected industry. Agricultural prosperity increases purchasing power. Without greater industrial production we cannot meet the demand for employment or goods. Nehru's policies, which we were following all these years, took science to our farmers and urged them to better their conditions. Thus have we been able to increase agricultural production from 72 million tonnes in 1966 to 121 million tonnes in 1976. If there is any ill-effect in some places, it is not because science is bad but because of over-enthusiasm, so that too much chemical fertilizer is used. There has to be a judicious mixture of old and new methods. In fact, the new should be used mainly to supplement the old, not to replace it entirely.

No path is easy and there are no short-cuts. We could have decided either to cling to the old or to sweep it away, but we chose the most difficult—a synthesis of the two. We have spanned many centuries to reach modern times. In the India of today, somewhere, sometimes you will find something from every period of its past history. In fact, it would not be too far from the truth to say that all the centuries co-exist. The sculptured Trimurti of Elephanta is just across the bay from Trombay where stands our first atomic plant. In some of our most ancient centres of religion and pilgrimage are some of the most modern factories of heavy electricals, power producing units or petrochemical complexes.

Our population has increased at an alarming rate, not because of the birth rate but because of better health and diminished infant mortality. The average life-span has grown from 27 years in 1947 to 61 in 1976. But let us remember that countries with a small fraction of the world population consume the bulk of the world's production of minerals, fossil fuels and so on. Thus we see that when it comes to the depletion of natural resources and environmental pollution, the increase of one inhabitant in an affluent country, at his level of living, is equivalent to an increase of many Asians, Africans or Latin Americans at their current material levels of living.

We have two types of pollution. The dirt of poverty and under-development and the fumes and grime of industry. Which is worse? Population and pollution have to be viewed within the total view of political, economic and social situations. No programme of population control can be effective without education and without a visible rise in the standard of living. To the very poor, every child is an earner and a helper.

These gigantic problems cannot be tackled without the willing cooperation of the people. Hence the necessity of a central authority which plans and guides and helps those in need, along with decentralization at different levels which could elicit the people's participation in the implementation of programmes and encourage local and individual initiative. In personal or national life, rights and privileges must be balanced with responsibilities.

One cannot be truly human and civilised unless one looks upon not only all fellowmen but all creation with the eyes of a friend. Since man first discovered that he could use nature for his own purposes he has been interfering with his environment. Man is a part of nature and only one of the many species who inhabit the earth. But he has treated it as a colony to exploit.

Must there be conflict between technology and a truly better world, or between enlightenment of the spirit and a higher standard of living? The inherent conflict is not between conservation and development, but between environment and the reckless exploitation of man and earth in the name of efficiency or profit. The fault lies not in science and technology as such, but in the sense of values of the contemporary world which ignores the rights of others and is oblivious of the longer perspective. We have to prove to the disinherited majority of the world that ecology and conservation will not work against their interest, but will bring an improvement in their lives. To withhold technology from them would deprive them of vast resources of energy and knowledge. This is no longer feasible nor will it be acceptable.

The environmental problems of developing countries are not the side-effects of excessive industrialisation, but reflect the inadequacy of development. Rich countries may look upon development as the cause of environment destruction, but to us it is one of the primary means of improving the environment for living or providing food, water, sanitation and shelter, of making the deserts green and the mountains habitable.

Our ancients were deeply concerned with ecology and advised that one should take from the earth and the atmosphere only as much as one put back into them. Such an ecological man was Tagore. I think of him as the most 'Indian' person I know, beautiful to look at, his eyes large pools of expression, his long hair, soft and flowing, his beard so typical of the sages of old. He established his university far from the city, not to be away from life but more fully in it. He was sensitive to beauty and to nature, but was at his most poignant when he touched upon the pain and inhumanity of man and the misery of poverty. He was Indian because he typified the values which we regard as especially ours—the vision and tolerance, the awareness of self as distinct and alone while remaining a part of everything else. And because of this awareness, he was a revolutionary. In his institutions in Santiniketan, he tried to revolutionise education. He created an atmosphere of peace in the midst of a myriad of activities—an attempt for civilization to return to its roots. And this is what he wanted for India too. His prayers concerned freedom from ignorance and superstition, from bigotry and narrowness.

What of the future? Change is a law of life and India will change. Some good may also be jettisoned along with some bad. But India, the essential India, will remain and our cultural traditions continue.

Spirituality cannot be locked in a compartment by itself. It cannot be shut on and off according to the occasion. It must be a part of one's living and one's being. Nor is spirituality in any way connected with poverty. Our great spiritual discoveries were made during periods of comparative affluence. The doctrines of detachment from possessions were developed not as a rationalisation of deprivation, but to prevent comfort and ease from dulling the senses. Spirituality means the enrichment of the spirit, the strengthening of one's inner resources and the stretching of one's range of experience. It is the ability to be still in the midst of activity and vibrantly alive in moments of calm: to accept joy and sorrow with the same equanimity. Perception and compassion are the marks of true spirituality.

Man, whether in India or elsewhere, has a long way to go to understand himself and to realise his potential and to come to terms with the universe, not as conqueror and exploiter but as partner and sharer.

In the meantime, we pray with Tagore:

'Where the mind is without fear and the head is held high;
Where knowledge is free;
Where the world has not been broken up into fragments by narrow domestic walls;
Where words come out from the depth of truth;
Where tireless striving stretches it arms toward perfection;
Where the clear stream of reason has not lost its way into the dreary desert sand of dead habit;
Where the mind is led forward by thee into ever-widening thought and action—
Into that heaven of freedom, my Father, let my country awake.'

250

GLOSSARY

Adi guru: the 'first guru' refers usually to the God Siva as the teacher of Parvati. Here it is used to refer to the first Shankar Acharya, saintly poet of the eighth century, the founder of the order that bears his name.

Advaita Vedanta: or the non-dualistic Vedanta. The Vedanta is the conclusion of the Veda. It presents a philosophical system originated by the legendary sage Vyasa that begins with the Upanishad: its approach goes by reasoning alone rather than by the rites of Ultimate Reality. The Advaita Vedanta teaches non-dualism or the identity of Relative and Absolute, of the Atman (limited understanding) and the Brahman (infinite understanding).

Agastya: a legendary sage born from the spontaneous ejaculation of Surya (Sun) and of Varuna (Ocean) at the sight of the nymph Urvashi. Among other things, tradition credits him with the introduction of Aryan institutions and ideas into the Dravidian south. In doing this, he arrested the growth of the Vindhya mountains that form a natural barrier between Northern India and the Deccan, and overcame, as told in the Râmâyana, all the demons of the South.

Ajanta: A few kilometers north-east of Aurangabad, the caves of Ajanta, consecrated to the Buddhist faith, cover some nine centuries of Indian art (from 200 B.C. to 700 A.D.) Twenty-nine caves burrow into a horseshoe cliff 600 meters above the river Vaghora. Six of them bear witness to the beauty of Indian painting of the classic period (400-500 A.D.)

Akbar: The third Moghul emperor and the true founder of the Moghul Empire and dynasty. During his reign, from 1555 to 1605, he conquered Dehli and Agra and extended his empire in the north of India, from the Himalayas to Narbada, from the Arab Ocean to the Gulf of Bengal. As a protector of the arts, he welcomed Hindu as well as Moslem artists to his court. A partisan of tolerance, he renounced the Islamic faith in 1582 to found a new, conciliatory religion that was not to survive him.

Ânandmayi Ma (Sri): Born in 1896 at Kheorta, Bengal. A great mystic, fervent believer of the Bhakti way, she devoted her life to the cult of the Goddess. She has several million followers who consider she is the reincarnation of the Devi. She has two ashrams, one in Benares, the other at Rishikesh.

Ardhanarishvara: 'the god who is half man' (and half woman). The hermaphrodite aspect of Siva-Shakti, the Supreme Being: the duality on which his Manifestation rests.

Arjuna: one of the five Pandava brothers, the hero of the Mahâbhârata. His dialogue with Krishna, before the great battle that is the high point of this epic poem, forms the eighteen chapters of the Bhagwad Gîtâ. He shares with his brothers the same wife, proud Draupadi, won in a tournament.

Âryabhata: an Indian mathematician and astronomer, born in 476. He wrote his great treatise, the Âryabhatîya, in Sanskrit. At the age of 23, he discovered the rotation of the world around the sun and the cause of eclipses. He taught trigonometry and algebra using very advanced methods in Pataliputra, now Patna, in Bihar. He was the author of five other works on mathematics, the measurement of time, the terrestrial sphere, etc.

Âryabhatîya: the works of the astronomer and mathematician Âryabhata. Four sections deal respectively with: a) astronomical numbers, b) mathematics, c) the measurement of time and the motion of the planets, d) the earthly globe and its relationship to the sun and the moon.

Arya Samaj: the 'Aryan Society' founded in Bombay in 1875 by Dayanand Sarasvati. Its aim was to return to the pure Vedic tradition of the Hymns.

Ashrama: hermitage, retreat; also the four (theoretical) steps in the life of a 'twice-born' man, belonging to the three highest castes, Brahman, Kshatriya and Vaishya, once he has received the sacred cord (upanayana).

Aurangzeb: the sixth emperor of the Moghul dynasty, born in 1659, died in 1707. He seized the throne by force after banishing his father, Shah Jahan, to life imprisonment and killing his three brothers. He reigned by violence and cruelty and practised religious intolerance, persecuting the Hindus and destroying their temples. He put to death the religious leader of the Sikhs, Guru Teg Bahadur, who refused to be converted to the Islamic faith.

Aurobindo (Sri): Aurobindo Ghose, born in Bengal in 1872, died in 1950. He first took part in the fight for independence, then devoted himself entirely to spiritual life in the ashram of Pondicherry, now Auroville. He published many half-philosophical, half-spiritual works, commentaries on the Veda and the Upanishad as well as poetry.

Baba Farid: Farid al-Din was born in 1175 at Khotwal, in the Punjab, of a noble Muslim family related to the king of Ghazni. He travelled to Mecca at the age of 16 and, a few years later, was initiated into Sufism by Kutab Din of Delhi. He settled in Jodhan, now Pak Pattan, where he died in 1265. A fervent mystic, he imposed cruel mortifications on himself. A saintly poet, he wrote 134 Punjabi hymns that were added to the Adi Granth, the Sikh Bible, by the Guru Nanak (see below) two centuries later. His tomb is a place of pilgrimage for Indians of all religions.

Bâna: a writer, considered as the last novelist of the Sanskrit tongue. He lived during the last half of the seventh century at the court of King Harsha Vardhana and became his biographer. His romantic biography, the Harshacharita, recreates all the pomp and splendour of a great Indian monarch. He is also the author of a famous fantastic novel: *Kadambari.*

Basava: the Brahman founder in the twelfth century of the sect of the Lingayat that denounced castes and the worship of idols. Born in 1106, died in 1167, he was the first minister of the principality of Kalyan, near Bombay.

Baz Bahadur: of the Turkish dynasty of the Khilji, Shah Bahadur, who lived in the second half of the sixth century, conquered Malwa, in the northwest part of what is now Madhya Pradesh. His fortified capital of Mandu, where he built remarkable structures, delights the visitor today. He fought courageously against Moghul emperor Akbar but once defeated, gave his allegiance to that potentate. A poet and a musician, he was so passionately in love with his Hindu wife, Rupmati, that it became a legend.

Besant, Annie: Born in London in October 1847, died in India in 1933. President of the Theosophical Society in 1907. Founder of the Indian Home Rule League in 1916. Author of numerous works, among them: *Religious Problems in India* and *How India forged her Freedom.*

Bhagwad Gîtâ: or song of the Blessed One, eighteen chapters of the sixth book of Mahâbhârata, the famous Indian epic poem. The date is not well defined; some believe that it was inserted in the Mahâbhârata at the time the Vishnu-Krishna cult developed; it probably goes back to the beginning of our era, at the latest about the fourth century.

Bharata (or Bharat): India's mythical founder, one of the four kings referred to in the Rig Veda. All the land between the oceans south of the Himalayas has been called Bharatavarsha for 'that is the dwelling-place of the descendants of Bharata' (Vishnu Purana). Bharata is also the name of a semi-legendary author who set down the first theories on poetry, dance, drama, music and aesthetics in general in a treatise concerning dramatic arts, the Natyashastra. This treatise, that dates back to the sixth century, may have been compiled from far more ancient works, of an encyclopaedic character.

Bhartrihari: a famed Sanskrit writer, poet, grammarian and philosopher. His best known work is the Bhattikavyam, a grammar treatise accompanied by learned comments on language. He lived in the seventh century.

Bhâskarâchârya: a remarkable mathematician and astronomer, born in 1114 at Bijapur, Deccan. In 1150, he wrote the famous treatise of mathematics entitled Siddhanta Shiromani. Written entirely in verse, the work is divided in four parts: the Leelavathi that deals with mathematics; the Bijaganita, that is devoted to algebra; the Grahaganitadhyaya, on astronomical calculations, and the Goladhyaya (theoretical astronomy).

Bhavabhuti: a great writer of the Sanskrit tongue. He lived at the court of the King of Kanauj towards 720-750. He wrote three plays, two of them relating in seven acts the legend of Rama:

the Mahaviracharita, based on the first songs of the Râmâyana, and the Uttararamacharita that tells of the exile of Sîtâ until his return. He excels in depicting conflicting sentiments, such as love and duty.

Bhikshu: a mendicant; a man who has abandoned all earthly possessions and must beg for subsistence; a Brahman who has reached the fourth stage of his life; a Buddhist monk.

Bose, Subhash Chandra: born on 23 January, 1897, in Orissa, of Bengali origin. He joined the Indian National Party in 1921 and was elected its president in 1938 and 1939, but was forced to resign because of his Nazi leanings. In 1941, he tried to form an alliance with the Axis in order to hasten India's freedom. He died in a flying accident while bound for Japan on 18 August, 1945.

Brahma: one of the Hindu trinity: Brahma-Vishnu-Siva. Brahma is the Creator of the universe. He is represented with four heads, holding the Veda, an ewer of lustral water, a rosary and ritual spoons, seated on a lotus that springs from the navel of Vishnu the Preserver.

Brahman: neutral word that means urge, development and is attributed to the Principle of all that is. In the Vedic hymns, the Brahman is the energy that links the officiating priest to the cosmic forces. In the Upanishads, the Brahman becomes the absolute Self, not to be conceived and not to be determined.

Brahman: a member of the first of the four Indian castes, dissolved by the Constitution of 1947. At first, the caste of Brahmins was only formed by priests and scholars. Today, only the Brahman may officiate at the rites in the temples and transmit sacred knowledge.

Brahmana: The Brahmana are a collection of works that describe the rules governing all the rites and their explanation. They compliment the four Vedas that were written far earlier. Their creation dates back to the seventh and eighth century. In the Brahmana are also found metaphysical and mystical treatises, called the Arnyaka, or books of the forest, that are intended to guide the contemplative life.

Brâhmo Samâj: society of the believer in Brahman, founded by Ram Mohun Roy in 1828, in which Christians, Moslems and Hindus met for common prayer. This form of oecumenism has been called Brahmoism.

Brihadaranyaka Upanishad: or the Great Upanishad of the Forest, so called because its teachings are essential and were transmitted in a retreat in the forest. The theme of this Upanishad is absolute identity of the Atman (individual conscience) with the Brahman (universal conscience, only Truth). This is discussed in the course of a lengthy debate between the enlightened kings, among them, the great Janaka; an ideal woman, Maitreyi; an insistant girl, Gargi and the sage, Yajnavalkya.

Brihadishvara: Brihat Ishvara, the Great God, one of the names given to Siva.

Buddha: from the word buddha meaning awake, enlightened, freed. An epithet given to prince Siddharta born in 500 B.C. in the clan of the Sakya, at Kapilavastu. He belonged to the caste of the Kshatriya and was also given the title of Sakyamuni, or sage of the Sakya. From the name of his family, he is also called Gautama. His death was about 420 B.C. He preached throughout the kingdom of Maghada, now Bihar, where it is possible to visit the sites of his first sermon (the gazelle park at Sarnath) and of his revelation (Bohd Gaya).

Chaitanya: mystical Bengali poet, born in 1485, died in 1533. Of a Brahmin family, he renounced the world at the age of 24 to preach a doctrine of love and devotion to Vishnu. He is the founder of Vishnavism in Bengal. He believed that it was possible to reach God only by total abandon to his power. Denying castes and sectarianism, he danced and sang his mystic poems throughout Orissa, Deccan and Bengal.

Chanda: a powerful demon, one of the generals of the army of Shumbha, chief of the Asura, killed by Kali who offered his decapitated head to the Great Goddess (seventh canto of the Devi Mahatmya).

Dayanand Saravati (Swami): born in 1824, died in 1883. He founded the Arya Samâj, in 1875, to protest against occidental influence in India. A distinguished writer of Sanskrit, he ignored the English language. He had an important role in the awakening of India.

Dakshinashvara: Dakshina Ishvara, the Lord who imparts teaching; one of the aspects of Siva, the ascetic, revealing the supreme truth to his disciples. This representation of Siva Dakshinamurti is mainly found in Southern India; in the North it takes the form of Lakulisha, Master of Wisdom.

Devi: the Great Goddess, the Mother, the Maya (Cosmic Illusion), the entire energy of the cosmos, the creative force. Devi appears under multiple forms: Durga, Kali, Ambika, Parvati, etc., but her ultimate reality is One.

Dharma: that which sustains, the way of life based on righteousness. The transcendental order that exists before creation: it is manifest later in the various states of the created being. The individual dharma is the rhythm of the development determined by the interior law rooted in the soul.

Draupadi: daughter of the King of Panchala, she was won in tournament by Arjuna, one of the five Pandava brothers. As the result of a vow with unexpected results, she became the common wife of all five brothers, the heroine of the Mahâbhârata.

Durga: the Great Goddess as a warrior maiden. The gods, unable to defeat Evil, together produce the 'teja' that condenses into a column of fire from which appears Durga, the conquering Virgin. Often shown fighting the demon buffalo, Mahishasura.

Elephanta: an island in the Harbour of Bombay, containing a vast excavated sanctuary dedicated to Siva and more specially to Maha Ishvara Murti, the representation of the triple aspect of the Great Lord: the creator, the destroyer and the preserver. It is the most perfect example of architecture and statuary of the post-Gupta period (sixth-eighth century).

Ellora: the site of Ellora, thirty kilometers from Aurangabad, includes thirty-four caves and a monolithic temple excavated along a platform set halfway up a nearly perpendicular cliff above the Deccan plateau. These sanctuaries and vihara were carved from the mid-sixth until the ninth century. The first are Buddhist, the next Brahman, the last Jain. By their quality, they form an unique group of the architecture and sculpture of the post-Gupta period.

Fahsien: the first Chinese pilgrim to visit India, at the beginning of the fifth century, following in the steps of Buddha. His memoirs, the Fo-kouo-ki, offer a remarkable view of India at the Gupta period.

Ganesh: Indian god of Wisdom, has some resemblance to Janus of the Romans. The son of Parvati, wife of Siva, he is shown with an elephant head (a sign of sagacity) riding on a rat (symbol of determination).

Gargi: the daughter of Vachaknavi. In the Brihadaranyaka Upanishad, she tires the sage Yajnavalkya with her constant questions on the ultimate reality of creation until he cries: 'You ask too many questions about an absolute that must go unquestioned. Do not ask too much, O Gargi.'

Gauri: the golden, one of the names of Parvati, wife of Siva. Parvati was dark-skinned, but by her austere practices, she lightened to a golden shade, hence the name.

Gayatri Mantra: a mantra of twenty-four syllables, divided into three verses of eight syllables each. The most sacred of all the Vedic mantras, considered the essence of the Hymns.

Gîtâ Govinda: the Song of the Shepherd. The Song of Songs of Sanskrit poetry. A long lyric poem dedicated to Krishna and his lovegames with beautiful Radha and her milkmaid companions, on the banks of the Jamuna. The author, Jayadeva, is held to be the last great Sanskrit poet (twelfth century).

Gondophermes: or Gondophares, an Indo-Parthian king who reigned in the North-west provinces of India (Gandhara Taxila, Kabul) between 20 and 48 of our era. Numismatic finds confirm the belief that it was his kingdom that was described by St Thomas in the account of his voyage to India.

Gupta: an Indian dynasty that reigned in the north of India from 320 to 510 A.D. Despite their belief in Hinduism, the Gupta were tolerant of other religions. As protectors of the arts, their reign fostered the richest and purest artistic and literary production of India. Considered the classic period.

Hiranyakasipu: a demon-king whose arrogance and impiety led him to challenge the sovereignty of world and sky. In his fourth incarnation as Narsingh, the lion-man, Vishnu opposed and slew him.

Huen-tsang: Chinese Buddhist pilgrim born in 600, died in 664, who travelled almost over the whole Indian peninsula from 630 to 645 in search of sacred writings. He saw the decline of Buddhism as well as the ruins left, in the North, by the passage of the Huns.

Indus civilization: important ruins of this civilization, that existed about 3000-1500 B.C., have been found along the Indus, mainly at Mohenjodaro, Harappa and Kathiavar. It was contemporary with the Euphrates civilization with which it established maritime connections. The remains show evidence of a pre-aryan culture with typical Dravidian cults of Siva and the Great Goddess, of yoni-linga (male and female organs), of the serpent and the tree that are still current today.

Jataka: the jataka (birth) is a series of tales composed in Pali about the previous lives of Buddha, telling about his successive rebirths in the animal kingdom until his reincarnation among human beings. They form part of the canon of early Buddhism and were inspired by ancient legends that were derived from even more ancient beliefs in which animals play an important part.

Jayadev: one of the last great Sanskrit poets. Born in the second half of the twelfth century, at Kindubilva, Bengal, he became the court poet of Bengal's last Hindu King. A fervent devotee of Krishna, he sings of the mystical loves of Krishna and Radha in the *Gîtâ Govinda*. This work is still very popular.

Kabir: an Indian poet of Moslem origin, born in 1440, died in 1518. He was one of the twelve disciples of a great mystic of syncretist leanings, Ramananda. The poems of Kabir, famous throughout Northern India, evoke the unity of all religions and denounce castes and cults.

Kali: 'Because you devour Kala (Time), you shall be called Kali'. Kali is the 'aroused' manifestation of Devi. She is linked to death and, thereby, to life. She is shown with a black skin, her tongue dripping with blood, brandishing a sword and a severed head, a garland of human skulls and a serpent around her neck.

Kâlidas: one of the best known names of Sanskrit literature. He probably lived at the end of the fourth and the beginning of the fifth century, and was attached to the court of King Vikramaditya. Three plays are attributed to him with some certainty: the famous *Ring of Shakuntala* and three long versified tales, unequalled examples of Mahakavya (long poem). The elegance of style and delicacy of sentiment are the perfect expression of the subtle beauty of India's classic period.

Kalpa: the time of a world's existence. One kalpa is but a day in the life of Brahma and lasts 4,320,000,000 earthly years. Each kalpa includes a thousand Mahayuga or Great Ages. Each Mahayuga in turn is divided into four yuga of decreasing length and quality. We are in the last phase of the present Mahayuga, called Kaliyuga, that is to last 432,000 years and which began in 3102 B.C.

Kalya: a mythic cobra belonging to the race of the Naga, the snakes that inhabit the Patala or Lower World. Kalya was poisoning the waters of Jamuna; Krishna vanquished him and banished him to the depths of the ocean.

Kapila: a half-legendary sage considered the founder of a philosophical and mystical system called Samkhya. This system (Darshana), of a dualistic and atheistic character, affirms that Spirit and Matter coexist from all eternity. Both Buddhism and Yoga have been inspired by the theories of Samkhya.

Karma: Karma is the act but also the law of the cause and effect of an act. Each act has a potential energy that releases a series of correlated effects. The karma does not only affect man, but all creation: the planets, the gods, and the animals all have their karma.

Kathâ: an exchange of words, and, by extension, tales and fables. The Kathâ is usually a tale with a moral where animals play the principal roles. The most ancient collection of Katha is the Brihat Kathâ (Great Tale) attributed to Gunadhya, that dates back to the first centuries of our era. The most famous is the Panchatantra.

Kathâ Sarit Sâgar: or an Ocean of Story, is the work of a Sivite brahman, Somadev, who lived in the eleventh century. This work seems a second version of the most ancient collection of tales, the Brihat Kathâ (see above). The main story is interwoven with 350 tales culled from Indian popular legends. Unlike most Kathâ, its aim is only to entertain.

Kaurava: the Kaurava are the hundred sons of the King of Hastinapura. Their rivalry and merciless war against their cousins, the five Pandava, are the central themes of the great epic poem: the Mahâbhârata (see below).

Khuzrau, Amir: Persian poet born at the end of the thirteenth century, died in 1325. A prolific author, he wrote both prose and poetry in Persian, Urdu and Avadhi (a Hindi dialect of the Benares region). He also composed music. Several sultans were his patrons in Delhi, where his tomb is still revered.

Konarak: a great temple of black stone in honor of Surya, the Sun God. The Sun Temple was in the form of a gigantic chariot with twelve wheels, drawn by seven horses. Only parts of the temple remain intact. It was built in the middle of the thirteenth century by a king of the Gangâ dynasty of Orissa, Narasimha, to commemorate his victory over Moslem invaders. Konarak is close to the holy city of Puri.

Krishna: the eighth reincarnation of Vishnu, came to destroy Kamsa, the tyrant demon, who had usurped the throne of Mathura. Born to the royal family of Mathura, as a baby Krishna was hidden from Kamsa with the shepherd Nanda. Brought up among the cowherds, he takes part in games of love with his companions, the milkmaids. These games, both erotic and mystic, are narrated in the Gîtâ Govinda of the poet Jayadeva. In the Mahâbhârata, Krishna leads the Pandava to victory after urging them to battle with teachings that are considered the quintessence of Hindu philosophy. These are set down in the Bhagwad Gîta.

Krishnamurti: Born in 1886 in Tamil Nadu. His spiritual powers were recognized at the age of nine by the theosophist, Leadbeater. The Theosophical Society under the leadership of Annie Besant sent him to study in London in 1910: she believed him to be a new Messiah. He rejected this role in 1929 and now preaches a doctrine of vacuity and refusal of any set creed.

Kural: 'Short piece', the work of the holy Tamil poet, Tiruvalluvar, is considered the 'fifth Veda' for its perfect form as well as its content. It runs for 1300 stanzas on the subjects of virtue, possessions and love. A masterpiece of Tamil literature, it is one of India's great books. The date of its conception is considered to lie between the third and the fifth century.

Lakshmî Devî: in the eighteenth century, commented with her husband, Balambhatta Vaidyanatha, on the Mitâkshara (see below), a set of laws, stressing women's right to property.

Leelavathi: the daughter and supposed collaborator of the great mathematician and astronomer of the twelfth century, Bhâskarâchârya (see above). In the first chapter of his book, the Siddhanta Shiromani, the author discusses mathematics with a bright young woman thought to be his daughter. That is why the chapter bears her name.

Lota: the brass jug used by the sadhu to drink from and perform their ablutions.

Mahabalipuram: about 50 kilometers south of Madras, is the ancient port of the Pallava, founded in 650, to serve as a sea outlet for their capital, Kanchipuram. Although the port has disappeared, the carved temples and rocks along the shore are intact. There are monolithic temples, caves with overhangs that shelter the sculptures and, in the open, two bas-reliefs representing the descent of the Ganges to earth and Krishna among the cowherds. The only building is the 'Shore Temple', a pyramid by the ocean's edge.

Mahâbhârata: great Sanskrit epic poem, attributed to the legendary sage Vyasa. It is composed of 100,000 verses of 32 syllables each. A collection of ancient tales and traditions, its compilation must have begun towards the fifth century B.C. It relates the rivalry and war of 100 Kaurava with their cousins, the five Pandava brothers, to seize the kingdom. All neighboring sovereigns as well as the gods take part in the battle held at Kurukshetra (in the Delhi region). The Pandava are victorious thanks to the advice of Krishna, who appears to them in the form of Vishvarupa, the Sovereign of the Universe, and stirs them to combat in the eighteen chapters of the Bhagwad Gîtâ. Shortly after their victory, the Pandava retire to the forest as hermits.

Mahâvîra: or Vardhamana Mahâvîra, the founder of Jainism, born to a noble Kshatriya family, in the Magadha, in the sixth century B.C. At the age of thirty he renounced the world and led the life of a wandering sage. He attained illumination and became a Jain (spiritual conqueror), and Mahâvîra (great hero). During the next thirty years, he preached his new doctrine along the region of the Ganges and founded a new order of ascetic monks. He died at the age of seventy in the Patna district. He seems to have been more of a reformer than a founder of the Jain faith. In the Jain hierarchy, there are twenty-four Thirthankars (pathmakers) or prophets. Mahâvîra is the last of the line.

Manu: the name of Manu is given to the first father of mankind as well as the fourteen who follow him and assume their role in each new cosmic period. To one of these Manu is attributed the Manu Samhita or Manu Code, whose origin goes back to the domination of Northern India by the Aryans. Under the form that has reached us, the Code of Manu dates back to 200 A.D. It is criticized for giving to the word varna, meaning colour, appearance, the sense of caste and in so doing, effectively hardening and systematising the caste system.

Markandeya Purana: one of the eighteen Purana named after the sage who is presumed to have written the text. The Markandeya Purana reveals the nature of Krishna, incarnation of Vishnu and relates some of the episodes of the Mahâbhârata in which Krishna plays an important part. The Devi Mahatmya, or the Acts of the Great Goddess, were inserted into it.

Matrika (the seven): the seven Mothers or Energies emitted by the Gods to aid the Great Goddess in her battle against the demons: Brahmani (force of Brahma), Mahashvari (energy of Siva), Kaumari (energy of Skanda), Vaishnavi (energy of Vishnu), Vahari (energy of Hari-Vishnu), Narasimhi (energy of one of Vishnu's incarnations), Aindri (energy of Indra).

Maurya: the longest dynasty that reigned on the vastest Empire that India had ever known before the foreign domination of the Moghuls. Their political, administrative and cultural system lasted from 322 to 185 B.C. Their greatest sovereign was Emperor Ashoka (273-232) whose laws engraved on stone remain a model of wise government.

Minakshi: the name of a deified daughter of a Pandya monarch, transformed into one of the aspects of the Great Goddess. She is worshipped in the great temple of Madura, dedicated both to her and to Siva, her husband under the name of Somasundara. Impressive rites accompanied by music are held in the temple each day.

Moghul (empire): the Empire of the Moghuls was founded in 1525 by Babur, a descendant of Tamerlane. Under the reign of Akbar (1555-1605) this dynasty of Turkish Moslem origin conquered all of Northern India and part of the Deccan district. At the end of the eighteenth century, the empire fell under the successive blows of the Sikh and Mahratta revolts, the Afghan raids and the first Europeans.

Muhammad Iqbal: a poet of the Persian and Urdu tongues, born at the beginning of the twentieth century at Lahore. His works are steeped in the philosophy of Islam. He died recently.

Muinuddin Chisti: the spiritual father of the Moghuls, this saintly Sufi poet lived in Ajmer, in the Rajasthan province, in the seventeenth century.

Munda: a powerful demon, one of the generals of the armies of Shumbha, leader of the Asura, killed by Kali who offered his decapitated head to the Great Goddess (seventh canto of the Devi Mahatmya).

Muruga: a mountain god, leader of the divinities of the first Dravidian beliefs. Adopted by Hinduism, he was assimilated into Skanda, son of Siva and leader of the celestial armies.

Naidu, Sarojini: born in Bengal in 1879. A talented poet and speaker, who became Governor of Uttar Pradesh in 1947 until her death in 1949.

Nanak (Guru): a disciple of Kabir and the first prophet of the Sikhs. He lived from 1469 to 1538. His teaching, close to that of Kabir, insists on divine unity, the futility of rituals and the absurdity of the caste system. His works, grouped with certain texts of Kabir and of other Moslem-Hindu saints form the bible of the Sikhs, the Adi Granth. Nine guru have come after Nanak, the last died in 1708.

Nârâyana (Guru): born at the end of the last century at Varkala, Kerala, died in 1928 in a state of samadhi (trance, the contemplation of the ultimate reality).

Nizam-Ud-din, Aulia: saintly Sufi poet, settled in Delhi under the reign of Akbar (sixth century). Highly respected during his life; a handsome mosque was built near his tomb in a quarter of Delhi that bears his name. In the same enclosure is the grave of the poet Khuzrau.

Noble, Margaret: an Irish woman, she met Swami Vivekânanda in London and became one of his first disciples. Initiated by Vivekânanda, whom she followed to India, she entered the order of Ramakrishna as Sister Niveditâ. She died in 1911, after writing the biography of Vivekânanda entitled *The Master as I saw Him.*

Onam (feast of): the greatest festival of Kerala lasts four days (end of August-beginning of September) right after the harvest. It is tied to the story of Asura Maha Bali who reigned in all three worlds, but allowed Vishnu—in the form of Vamana, the dwarf—to reconquer them by ruse. This regard for the rules of cosmic 'fair play' won him Vishnu's permission to return once every year to his former terrestrial domains. In the rejoicing of Onam, the Keralites celebrate the annual return of Maha Bali.

Panchatantra: a famous collection of tales and fables with a moral ending, in five volumes. It is not known when they were written, but the date is situated between the third and the fourth century. There are several versions. This didactic work, probably intended for the education of a young prince, was set down in verse and prose. Its characters are animals that talk like human beings. Both Grimm and La Fontaine found inspiration in the Panchatantra.

Pandava: the five supposed sons of Pandu, the king of Indraprastha, near the actual Delhi. Victims of their cousins, the hundred Kaurava, who robbed them of their kingdom, and of their common wife, Draupadi, in a game of loaded dice. Their struggle to reconquer their heritage forms the central theme of the great Indian epic the Mahâbhârata (see above).

Parvati: one aspect of the Great Goddess. Parvati is the daughter of the Himalaya and the wife of Siva. She is also the mother of Ganesh, the god with the elephant head.

Pipal or Pippala: Ficus reliogiosa, the latex tree quoted in the Veda and the Chandogya Upanishad. As a tree of Paradise, it makes the Soma rain and grows in the heaven of the gods. Siva, the preserver of the energy forces of the cosmos meditates under a Pipal, and it is under a Pipal that Sakya muni has his revelation and becomes Buddha.

Purana: the name given to a category of sacred texts attributed to the legendary sage Vyasa. They form an entire set of teachings bearing on cosmogony, theogony, mythical and semi-recorded history. The Purana mark the development of a certain deism where the cults of Siva, Vishnu and the Great Goddess are predominant. There are eighteen Purana generally recognized in Northern India out of a total of thirty-six. The most ancient date back to the fourth century B.C. but modifications were added until the fifteenth century.

Pushkar: a huge camel fair held each year in October or November; a pilgrimage held at the same time. Pushkar is situated 11 kilometers from Ajmer, the Moslem holy city of Rajasthan. A camel race is held in the great arena of the fair.

Radha: a young milkmaid, the heroine of the Gîtâ Govinda. Her passionate love-making with Krishna, in the forest of Vrindavana, on the banks of Jamuna, evokes the transports and the torments of the soul searching for the Absolute. Radha's love for the shepherd-God has constantly inspired Indian artists and writers.

Raghunathji: of Raghunatha, the Lord of the Raghu. A mythical ancestor of Rama, the incarnation of Vishnu, Raghunathji is a particular aspect of the adoration of Vishnu-Rama during the great festival of Dusserah each autumn.

Rama Chandra: the seventh incarnation of Vishnu, descended to earth as Rama to deliver the world from evil. But the main object of this avatar was to free Sîtâ, ideal wife of Rama, kidnapped by the demon Ravana who held her a prisoner in the island of Lanka (Ceylon). The capture and the liberation of Sîtâ are the themes of the great epic poem, Râmâyana.

Ramakrishna Paramahansa: a great Indian mystic born in 1836 to a poor Brahmin family, died in 1886. Non-sectarian and inspired prophet, his teachings culminate in the cult of the Mother. Among his most famous disciples was Vivekânanda.

Râmâyana: or the Song of Rama, one of the two Sanskrit epic poems, attributed to Valmiki who assembled traditional legends that had come down orally into a poetic composition. Shorter than the Mahâbhârata, the Râmâyana is composed of 24,000 stanzas in seven volumes; far less archaic and showing more unity, it is centered on the adventures of Rama and his struggle with the demon Ravana to recover his wife, Sîtâ. The fine style led the way for courtly poetry.

Ram Mohun Roy, rajah: founder of the Brâhmo Samâj, born in a famous Brahmin family of Western Bengal in 1772. His numerous works in Persian, Bengali and English ushered in the contemporary era of India. Ram Mohun Roy died in 1833 in

Bristol. His ideal of liberty that transcended race and religion made him a passionate observer of the French Revolution, the South-American revolution of 1823 and the Reform Movement in England of the 1830s.

Ravana: a powerful demon, the lord of the isle of Lanka (Ceylon). One of the main characters of the Râmâyana, he carried off Sîtâ, the wife of Rama and held her captive on his island. Since his ten heads grew back as fast as they were hacked off, he was killed by an arrow of heavenly fire shot by Rama.

Rig Veda: the first and most ancient of the Vedas, composed by several legendary rishi whose names are connected to the hymns. The Rig Veda is in fact a huge fresco of the religious, economical, social and political life of the Aryans in Northern India; it was composed over a period of time from 1500 to 500 B.C. More than a thousand hymns are dedicated to glorifying the divinities protecting cults, to cosmogony and metaphysical speculations. Among all the hymns devoted to the origins of the universe, the hymn to creation is considered to be the most ancient example of Aryan philosophical thought.

Rishi: the rishi are the great sages to whom the Vedic hymns and sacred writings were revealed. Vyasa and Agastya are among the best known rishi.

Sandhya: the prayer each high-caste Hindu must recite morning, noon and night.

Sankalpa: a solemn vow. The intention is personified in the son of Sam-Kalpa and Brahma.

Sârangî: India's main string-instrument, formed of a cylinder and its handle. Thirteen strings are placed under three or four gut strings. The instrument is played with a short arc-shaped bow.

Saravastî: Goddess of eloquence, music, science and learning in general. She is represented as a fair-skinned young woman, enthroned on a lotus, bearing lotus flowers, a vina and the Veda. Her vehicle is a swan.

Sarod: one of the most resonant musical instruments of India, in the shape of a half sphere with a handle almost as wide as the body. It is covered with a sheet of metal that served as a finger board. Its four melodic strings and the resonant strings are played with metal-sheathed fingers.

Shanâî: an oboe-like instrument. The main part consists of a conic shaped tube pierced with holes. The larger end widens into a bell shape, the narrower end is closed by a copper mouthpiece pierced by two reeds held by a string.

Shankara: The bringer of good, beneficial. One of the epithets given to Siva, as well as certain saints.

Shankarâchârya: or the Master who appeases. An epithet of Siva that is also given to a saintly poet born in Kerala around 700, the author of a considerable number of sacred texts and mystical poems. He is, with Gaudapada, the leader of the Advaita-Vedanta school of philosophy (see above). He founded a religious order whose spiritual leaders bear his name.

Shvetâshvatara Upanishad: a short Upanishad of some 113 verses in 6 chapters. It is named after the wise man Shvetâshvatara (he who controls himself), believed to be its author. In a synthesis of the main Hindu beliefs, it replies to the great questions of life: what is the meaning of the Universe, where does it come from, why are we born, what is the object of life?

Siva: Siva is one aspect of the Hindu trinity that includes Brahma, the Creator, Vishnu the Preserver and Siva the Destroyer. Of ancient origin (his effigy is set in the seals of the Indus) his importance among the Hindu divinities grows as grow the legends of the gods gathered in the Purana. In medieval Hinduism, he plays a most important role, particularly in certain Tantric teachings where he becomes the Absolute.

Siva linga: the linga is a more or less abstract symbol of the phallus—signifying dynamic and creative force—through destruction comes creation. The linga is usually shown deep in the yoni, or vagina of the Goddess. In the Sivite temples, the linga is in the holy of holies, under the huge tower of the sanctuary that magnifies its form.

Sivaji: Sivaji Bhonsla, a Mahratta born in 1627, died in 1680. Both chivalrous and religious, he fought for the revival of Hinduism and against foreign Moslem occupation. He used the songs of the holy bhakti of the Maharashtra to galvanize the rough mountain men who formed the bulk of his troops.

Sîtâ: the furrow. Janaka, king of Mithila, her supposed father, saw her spring forth from a furrow as he ploughed his fields. The wife of Rama (Vishnu's seventh incarnation) she is the heroine of the Râmâyana. Carried off by Ravana, the ten-headed Demon, to his isle of Lanka, she was won back after a hard battle. To quell doubts about her chastity while she was Ravana's captive, she was forced to undergo trial by fire. She emerged victorious from this test. Towards the end of her life, she returned to the bosom of the earth from which she had sprung. She is the perfect wife: brave, proud and pure.

Sitâr: the invention of the sitar is attributed to poet Amir Khuzrau in the fourteenth century. It is formed by a cylindrical sound box fixed on a long handle. On this handle mobile keys slide along runners. On the top of the box, four steel and copper strings are maintained in place by an ivory holder. Two more strings are set on each side. Other resonant strings are strung below. The player strums the strings with a metal plectrum.

Somadeva: A Sivite brahman of Kashmir, who wrote the Kathâ Sarit Sagâr (see above) from 1063 to 1081, at the court of King Ananta for the entertainment of his wife, Princess Suryamati. His simple but elegant style makes him one of the great Sanskrit authors.

Somanâtha: name of a famous linga of Siva and the place where it was set up by the god Soma, a divinity that symbolises a special drink offered in libation to the gods, occasionally identified with the moon (Chandra). The name of Somanâtha was first given to one of the twelve great temples sheltering the twelve lingas; then by extension to a number of Siva linga sanctuaries.

Tagore, Rabindranath: born in 1861 to a rich brahmin family of Bengal. He studied in England and very soon began to publish books and verse. He was awarded a Nobel prize in 1913. Besides his literary work—mostly lyrical—he founded in Bengal the University of Shantiniketan (dwelling of peace) where he upheld both occidental and oriental values. Tagore died in 1941.

Thiruvalluvar: holy poet, probably the most famous Tamil author. His book, the Kural, is considered by many the fifth Veda. The events of his life are legendary. He is said to have been of a lower caste family, a weaver like Kabir and must have lived toward the end of the third Sangram (an academy of learning founded by the Pandya) in which the Kural was crowned with success (about the third century).

Trimûrti: a triad. Describes the triple aspect of the Hindu trinity (Brahma, Vishnu, Shiva). For the Sivites, there is also a trimûrti of Siva where he is represented as unchanging in the centre, with his terrifying aspect (Aghora) on the right, and his seductive feminine aspect (Shakti and Maya) at the left. This trimûrti is carved on the temple-cave of Elephanta.

Tulsi: Ocimum sanctum, one of the sixty different kinds of basil found in hot climates. Particularly revered by the followers of Vishnu. Legends tell that a woman had entered the monastic life only to become Vishnu's bride. As a revenge, the goddess Lakshmî, changed her into a plant bearing her name. The tulsi is mentioned in the Purana as one of the ingredients in making the liquor of immortality: Amrita.

Upanishads: philosophical essays often presented as dialogues between teacher and disciples. Composed in the sixth century B.C., the Upanishads develop most of the philosophical and spiritual content of the Veda, while denouncing ritualism. They open the way to pure metaphysics. There are 108 Upanishads: their teachings were a capital influence on the development of Indian thought and the basis of the two great Hindu schools of philosophy: the Vedanta and the Samkhya.

Valmiki: a semi-legendary author of the great epic, Râmâyana, called Adi Kavi, or the first poet. The legend says that once a thief and a hunter he was converted by brahmins. After hearing the story of Rama, encouraged by Brahma himself, he underwent a period of austerity in order to become worthy to relate this story. Once purified by ascetic practices, he wrote the epic of Rama in inspired verse.

Veda: the Veda is the total of sacred knowledge revealed to mankind. It is made up of texts of several different eras: the four Veda (Indo-Aryan spiritual experiences, myths, beliefs and rituals): the Rig Veda, the Yajur Veda, the Soma Veda and the Atharva Veda; the writings that followed and reveal the speculative and imaginative Indian spirit: the Aranyaka, the Upanishad, the Ithasa or epic poems, and the Purana. According to some, the Tantra form the last part of the Veda.

Vihara: a monastery with a central hall for assembly and cells on each side for the members of a religious order.

Vedanta: the conclusion or essence of Veda. The name is given to the second and most important part of the Mimamsa, or the philosophical speculations that include the teachings of the Upanishad, the Bagwad Gîtâ and the Brahma sutra. Its tendancy is to teach that the known Universe is identical in its essence to the non-manifest Absolute. The mythical founder of this metaphysical system is the sage, Vyasa, but others, like the great philosopher and critic, Shankarâchârya, and later, Ramanuja, developed it further and gave it structure.

Veenâ: a string instrument that is considered the most subtle of all. The veenâ is formed by two dried gourds fixed on a hollowed bamboo tube that give it resonance. Twenty-two keys are mounted in wax on the bamboo finger board. There are seven strings, four above and three on the side. The strings are plucked with metal plectrums. This type of veenâ is called Sarasvati veenâ, or veenâ from the North. There is another kind in the South, called the Rudra veenâ.

Vinoba Bhave: of Mahratta descent, born in 1895. A disciple of Gandhi, he is now considered his successor. He owns an ashram in Madhya Pradesh. Like Gandhi, he seeks individual and social reforms, but has added new orientations.

Vishnu: the second of the Hindu trinity: Brahma the creator, Vishnu the preserver, Siva the destroyer. In order to protect creation from the catastrophes that menace the world—especially the attacks of demonic forces—Vishnu was forced to reincarnate himself throughout the ages. Of all ten principal incarnations, the two most famous ones are these of Rama (sung in the Râmâyana) and of Krishna (told in the Mahâbhârata with the Bhagwad Gîtâ and the Govinda Gîtâ.) The Purana that tell the story of Vishnu are the Vishnu Purana, the Bhagavata Purana, the Garuda Purana, the Markandeya Purana, the Padma Purana and the Vahara Purana.

Vishvarupa: he who assumes all forms. Vishnu-Krishna, in the aspect of the Lord of the Universe, both origin and support of all creation. This aspect often represented in Indian paintings and sculpture is described at the end of the Bhagwad Gîtâ.

Vivekânanda, Swami: religious name of Narendranath Datta, born in Calcutta in 1862, of a noble Bengali family, died there in 1902. A disciple of Ramakrishna, he is the author of numerous works founded on the Vedanta.

Vratya Stoma: or prayer (hymns) for the Vratya. This ceremony is quoted in the Atharva Veda as a ritual of integration of the Vratya in the brahmanic system of castes, specially by marriage. The Vratya were an aboriginal religious community, adorers of Siva Rudra, with semi-heretical practices, that were influential in the Indian Ganges region. Their importance led the Brahmans to find some way to integrate them in their social system. It would seem that the noble family of Licchavi, settled in what is now Bihar since the seventh century B.C., and from which descended Gautama Buddha and the Gupta dynasty, belonged to this community.

Yogi: A yogi practices the yoga discipline based on the Yoga Sutra of Patanjali or on other systems of Yoga. Composed in the fourth century, the Yoga Sutras of Patanjali teach the exercises necessary to reach concentration of the mind, control of body and specially of breathing, and finally union with the Supreme Reality. By such concentration and control, the yogi arrests the unceasing movement of the intellect and realizes his true nature that is one with the Absolute. Patanjali himself describes the eight steps of yoga needed to reach deliverance or freedom from reincarnation. Certain supernatural powers can be acquired by the yogi, whose Master is Siva.